WANDA E. BRUNSTETTER'S

Amish Friends

HARVEST

COOKBOOK

*Over 240 Recipes for Using and Preserving
the Bounty of the Land*

SHILOH RUN PRESS

An Imprint of Barbour Publishing, Inc.

Published by Shiloh Run Press, an imprint of Barbour Publishing, Inc., P.O. Box 719, Uhrichsville, OH 44683, www.shilohrunpress.com

Our mission is to publish and distribute inspirational products offering exceptional value and biblical encouragement to the masses.

 Member of the
Evangelical Christian
Publishers Association

Printed in China.

INTRODUCTION and ACKNOWLEDGMENTS

We reached out to the folks of various plain communities through *The Budget* newspaper as well as my numerous contacts within the communities of Amish and Mennonites. The Barbour staff and I thank all who generously supplied their recipes and gardening tips. Special thanks to Mary Alice Yoder for providing her own story of growing up with a garden.

The intention for this cookbook is to encourage the practice of home gardening, eating fresh produce, and preserving the harvest for those seasons when fresh and local foods are hard to come by.

May you be inspired,

Wanda E. Brunstetter

TABLE of CONTENTS

To every thing there is a season, and a time to every purpose under the heaven: A time to be born, and a time to die; a time to plant, and a time to pluck up that which is planted;

ECCLESIASTES 3:1–2

Reflections on the Amish Family Garden
By Mary Alice Yoder of Topeka, Indiana

When I think about what my garden means to me, it is hard to put to words. Growing up, a garden was such a large part of my life that it goes hand in hand with having a bed to sleep in. A garden to an Amish child is like a bicycle was to an "English" child. It was there every summer, not ever a question of how or why. I recall helping my grandmother put seeds into the ground at age five.

A garden is a family project. Not only for the girls, but boys and men as well. Daddy plowed the garden in spring, and as soon as the weather permitted, we planted peas, lettuce, and radishes, maybe onions as well. On the 100th day of the year you were to plant potatoes. But often Grandma would come out of her little house and tell us that today was not a good sign for root crops. Sometimes we went on anyways; sometimes we waited.

Soon came the time to add beans, beets, kohlrabi, cabbage, cucumbers, tomatoes, and corn. Every year we dreaded the long harvest of strawberries, because when we picked them it was wet and we got a backache.

I have many memories stored from the garden. There is one vivid memory of laying in the pea row, snitching fresh peas so tender they melted right into my throat. Or picking up potatoes and throwing a little one at my pesky big brother. Or riding the big Belgian horse hitched to the cultivator. Not to mention the times we grumbled due to the big long rows of beans to pick.

Also the Amish garden is an important part of Amish life because we have to can as many vegetables as we'll need and freeze lots of corn. Store-bought sweet corn isn't near as good as the stuff from your own garden. When we host church at our house, we serve home-canned pickles and red beets along with some canned jelly or frozen strawberry jam. Having to buy these things from a store would seem wasteful of our money.

Amish gardens almost always have some flowers as well. Color appeals to most women, and having it in flowers is fine and dandy. We plant lots of annuals that we gather seeds from for next year. Sometimes we have made nice paths through the garden and have a fancy circle of flowers. Digging canna bulbs and dahlias was a normal fall job for me.

Instilled into our roots is a very deep respect for a garden. Even a "pride" in being able to grow all kinds of crops. We do it *just like mom did*— for the most part.

Advice from Amish Gardeners

He that gathereth in summer is a wise son:
but he that sleepeth in harvest is a
son that causeth shame.

Proverbs 10:5

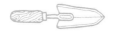

What are your tips for strong and healthy plants that produce a good harvest?

PLANTING BY THE SIGNS

- ◆ When crocuses come up, start your eggplant and peppers inside. Don't plant outside until the tall iris bloom.
- ◆ Start tomatoes inside when daffodils start to come up. Plant outside when the lily of the valley or the lilacs start to bloom.
- ◆ Watch your lilac bushes. When the leaves start to burst out, plant your root crops, peas, lettuce, and cabbage outside. When the lilacs are in full bloom, it is often safe to plant corn and beans.
- ◆ Start the late cabbage crop when the blackberries bloom.

Ruth Hochstettler, Dundee, OH

ASPARAGUS

Apply plenty of salt and wood ashes during the winter for nice stalks of asparagus.

Mary E. Miller, Middlebury, IN

SPRING TONIC FOR GRAPES

1 gallon water	1 handful salt
1 handful sulfur	1 handful lime

Mix well. Make a small cavity around the grape vine and pour this over stalk and into hole. Makes enough for 1 plant.

Rachel Yoder, Burton, OH

PLANT FOOD FOR RASPBERRY OR GRAPE PLANTS

1 gallon white lime or wood ashes
1 handful Epsom salt

Mix the lime and salt well and spread a large handful around each plant in February, March, and April, and also in the fall.

Katie Zook, Apple Creek, OH

FRUIT TREE FERTILIZER

100 pounds wood ashes
50 pounds lime

25 pounds sulfur
12 pounds salt

Mix well. Spade in ground around fruit trees. Also apply lime as far around the trees as the branches reach. Preferably just before it rains.

Wollie Schlabach, Smicksburg, PA

LETTUCE

For healthier, tastier lettuce, sprinkle some blood meal in the rows where the seeds are planted.

Mary E. Miller, Middlebury, IN

MILK FORTIFIER

Whenever you have extra or sour milk, dilute it with water and put on your vegetable plants. It is also good for raspberry plants.

Martha Miller, Edgar, WI

PLANTING PICKLES

Plant your pickle/cucumber seeds on the first day of summer (June 21) for a fast and good growing crop. By then your early garden produce will be done and you'll have space for the pickles.

Emma Miller, Baltic, OH

PLANTING POTATOES

Before planting, coat the seed potatoes in sulfur and/or lime. Spray potato plants with Basic H (from Shaklee) diluted in water for better yields.

Mrs. Raymond Kauffman, Laplata, MO

PLANTING TOMATOES

Choose a healthy plant to start. Dig a deep hole and add 1 teaspoon dry cement and 1 teaspoon Epsom salt. Set plant so that only top branches are out of the hole. Water. Fill hole with dirt. You'll have lots of tomatoes.

Barbara Beechy, Manawa, WI

TOMATO SWEETENER

For sweeter-tasting tomatoes, dig a hole for your plant and add 2 tablespoons Epsom salt and 1/3 cup lime. Mix into loose soil, then plant your tomato.

Sarah W. Hershberger, McKenzie, TN

TOMATO FERTILIZER

1 tablespoon Epsom salt
1 tablespoon baking powder
1 gallon water

1 teaspoon saltpeter
1 teaspoon ammonia

Mix and pour 1 quart of the mixture on each plant. Apply once per month. Can also be used on flowers.

Barbara Beechy, Manawa, WI

PLANT FOOD

1 teaspoon cream of tartar
1 teaspoon saltpeter
1 teaspoon ammonia

1 teaspoon Epsom salt
1 gallon warm water

Mix all ingredients together. Give to plants once a month.

Rose Marie Shetler, Berne, IN

BONE MEAL

Bone meal works well when spread by hand around berry patches. It keeps away bugs while feeding the plants.

Vera Mast, Kalona, IA

EGG SHELL BOOSTER

To encourage flowers to grow and bloom, soak egg shells in warm water. Use the water on the plants.

Ruth Hochstettler, Dundee, OH

Beautiful Flowers

3 cups triple 20
1 cup 9-15-30

$1/8$ cup clear liquid soap
2 gallons water

Mix. Can give this to petunias every day. For other flowers, use once or twice a week.

Leona Mullet, Burton, OH

Weed Blocker

After your plants are up, layer flattened cardboard boxes around your plants or in the rows and cover with mulch of straw, old hay, aged manure, compost, or the like. It really helps with controlling weeds and maintaining moisture.

Elizabeth Shetler, Brinkhaven, OH

If You Can't Beat the Weeds, Eat Them

Some of what we call weeds today are garden plants brought to America by our immigrating ancestors. Finding an inviting environment, these plants made themselves at home, taking over in many places. Caution: Always know what you have before eating.

PLANTAIN
A medicinal plant. If stung in the garden, chew a leaf of plantain and apply the paste to the bite.

DANDELION
Nutritious and medicinal—the root, stems, leaves, and flowers can all be eaten. Dry the roots for a coffee substitute. Fix young leaves as greens. Add flowers to a salad or deep fry. Jelly and wine are also made from the flowers.

PURSLANE
Very nutritious and a sign that your garden soil is rich. Add leaves to salads.

LAMB'S-QUARTERS
A wild spinachlike leaf that grows on tall stalks. Use anywhere you use spinach, though is preferable cooked.

OXALIS (WOOD SORREL)
Oxalis is an edible plant with leaves that look like clover. Has a lemony flavor; good in salads, soups, and stews.

VIOLETS
Leaves and flowers are great salad garnish with mild flavor. Violet flowers make lovely jelly.

GARLIC MUSTARD
Leaves are most commonly eaten near first frost when they are less bitter.

STINGING NETTLES
Extremely nutritious with medicinal uses. Cook the leaves to destroy the stingers and add to soups. Dry the leaves and make tea.

How do you deal with bugs in the garden that threaten the harvest?

ORGANIC BUG SPRAY

1 pint household ammonia
1 pint black strap molasses
1 pint hydrogen peroxide

2 cups apple cider vinegar
5 gallons water

Mix and spray the bugs away.

Lydia C. Yoder, Chetopa, KS

INSECT REPELLENT

1 cup Shaklee's Basic H
16 milliliters Tempo
(available from vet clinic)

2 gallons water

Mix in a sprayer and use to spray lawns and outdoor areas before parties or other gatherings. Double the amount of Tempo to spray around doorways and windows that will be left open.

Susanna Mast, Kalona, IA

FOR BUGS ON ROSES

1 teaspoon Ivory dish soap
1 tablespoon baking soda

1 gallon water

Mix and spray on plants.

Katie Zook, Apple Creek, OH

Fly Spray

3 cups water
2 cups white vinegar

1 cup Skin So Soft (Avon product)
1 tablespoon citronella or eucalyptus oil

Put in spray bottle and shake well. Spray table before setting. It is not poisonous, and it really works.

Leona Mullet, Burton, OH

Horse Fly Spray

2 cups Dawn dish soap
4 cups white vinegar

2 cups kerosene
6 cups water

Mix all together and put in spray bottle. We pick this over store-bought spray.

Enos and Lydia Yoder, Fredericksburg, OH

Fruit Fly Trap

1 tablespoon cider vinegar
6 drops dish detergent

¼ cup water

Mix together in a small container. Let sit uncovered on the counter. The bugs will fly in, but they won't come out.

Thelma Zook, Oakland, MD

CABBAGE WORMS

To keep worms away from cabbage plants, mix garlic powder, red pepper flakes, and flour. Sprinkle over plants when heads start to form.

Mrs. Freeman Yoder, Millersburg, OH

BUGGY BEANS

To keep bugs off beans, mix 2 cups sorghum molasses with 1 gallon water and spray until leaves are wet. Repeat after each rain.

Mrs. Raymond Kauffman, Laplata, MO

BASIL AND TOMATOES

Plant basil among tomatoes. Basil may ward off bugs and improve the flavor of the tomatoes.

RADISH WORMS

When planting radishes, put coffee grounds or black pepper in with the seeds to keep worms away.

Mrs. Freeman Yoder, Millersburg, OH

APHID REMEDY

For aphids on vegetable plants, spray with a strong solution of Ivory dish soap mixed in water.

Sarah W. Hershberger, McKenzie, TN

JUNE BUGS

Adding lime to your garden and yard will discourage June bugs from laying their eggs.

Christina Peight, Belleville, PA

POTATO BUGS

Put Epsom salt on the rows with the potatoes as you plant them to prevent bugs.

Lorene Helmuth, Junction City, WI

SQUASH BUGS

To combat squash bugs that seem to strike just as you think you might get a good crop, dip the seeds briefly into untreated kerosene before planting. It will also work for Chinese cabbage seeds.

Alvin and Katie Hertzler, Salisbury, PA

BUG BAND

Tie a piece of baler twine (not the plastic) around your neck and around your wrist or ankle. It will keep the bugs away.

Katie W. Yoder, Goshen, IN

MOTHBALL DEFENDERS

Scatter mothballs by hand on the ground around trees to prevent worms in fruit. May also help prevent blight on scrubs and vines.

Vera Mast, Kalona, IA

ANT BLOCK

To stop ants from invading your kitchen, simply wash and spray countertops, cabinets, and floors with equal parts of vinegar and water.

Mary E. Miller, Middlebury, IN

MILK BATH

Diluted milk will keep mites off houseplants and outdoor plants.

Vera Mast, Kalona, IA

FRUIT TREE BUG TRAPS

Combine water, apple cider vinegar, and sugar. Pour into a heavy plastic jug with a handle loop to tie twine around. Fill only about ¼ full, and add a banana peel to each jug. Hang in the middle of the tree as best you can reach. Refresh the contents when it fills with bugs. Large trees may require more than one jug.

Marigold Guardians

Plant marigolds around your cucumbers, squash, and melons. The marigolds help to keep the bugs away while brightening your garden.

Sarah W. Hershberger, McKenzie, TN

Companion Herbs

Plant dill among cabbage to attract beneficial bugs that will help control the pests. Plant or mulch with mint around members of the cabbage (*brassica*) family to deter bugs. Chamomile, chives, oregano, rosemary, sage, and thyme are all beneficial to cabbage.

Pantry Bugs

To keep bugs out of flour and other grains, tape a bay leaf inside the bag or canister lid, but not touching the flour.

Sugar Tonic

To kill bugs and worms in the garden, sprinkle plants with water, then sprinkle with white sugar.

Viola Beechy, Manawa, WI

Poison Ivy

To remove poison ivy, mix together 1 gallon soapy water and 3 pounds salt. Spray area well.

Edith Mast, Bertha, MN

How do you deal with disease in the garden?

BANANA PEELS

Put a banana peel in the hole when you first plant a tomato. Helps prevent blight.

Barbara Beechy, Manawa, WI

BLIGHT FORMULA

1 tablespoon Epsom salt
1 tablespoon saltpeter
1 tablespoon baking powder
1 teaspoon ammonia or dish soap
1 gallon water (optional)

Combine and give 1 part mixture to each plant every 2 weeks or spray heavily.

For tomatoes, start using in spring until plants are big and full of green tomatoes. It may also be used on cucumbers, melons, peas, or any plant showing blight.

It can also be used to fertilize. For peas, add more Epsom salt.

Anna Yoder, Fairchild, WI

TOMATO BLIGHT SPRAY

2 cups raw whole milk
⅓ cup sugar
⅓ cup Epsom salt
1 gallon water

Combine and spray plants once a week for prevention. If you have a problem with blight, spray twice a week. It won't completely cure the problem, but it will help.

Mrs. Raymond Kauffman, Laplata, MO

Tomato Blight Spray #2

1 gallon water
1 tablespoon saltpeter

1 tablespoon baking powder
1 teaspoon ammonia

Mix well and give 2 cups per plant every 2 weeks.

Martha Miller, Edgar, WI

Rotting Pepper Remedy

1½ tablespoons 35% peroxide
  (food grade)

1 tablespoon sugar
1 gallon water

Mix and spray the plant with it. It stopped the rotting right away for me. Also good to use on your strawberry plants.

Wollie Schlabach, Smicksburg, PA

Powdery Mildew Control

4 tablespoons baking soda
2 tablespoons Murphy's Oil
  soap

1 gallon warm water

Mix ingredients and pour into a handheld mist sprayer. Apply liberally as soon as you see telltale white spots on your perennials.

Ruth Hochstettler, Dundee, OH

What are your tips for harvesttime?

CELERY

To keep celery crisp, stand it up in a pitcher of cold, salted water and refrigerate.

Barbara Troyer, Millersburg, OH

GARLIC

Garlic should be stored in a dry, airy place away from light. Garlic cloves can be kept in the freezer. When ready to use, chop before thawing. Garlic buds will never dry out if stored in a bottle of cooking oil, and when the garlic's gone, you can use oil for salads

Betty Miller, Goshen, IN

GREEN TOMATOES

Wrap green tomatoes in newspaper and store in a cool, dark place and they will ripen nicely.

Mrs. Levi O. Schwartz, Berne, IN

LEMONS

Store whole lemons in a closed jar of water in the fridge, and when you juice them they will yield more juice.

Betty Miller, Goshen, IN

Lettuce Salads

When preparing a salad with leafy greens and watery vegetables ahead of time, first place a small plate upside down in the bottom of the serving bowl. Any moisture that weeps from the vegetables will run under the plate, and the vegetables will stay fresh and crisp.

Potatoes

Potatoes will keep longer if kept in a cool, dry place, stored in a brown paper bag.

Betty Miller, Goshen, IN

Storing Vegetables

Most fruits and vegetables store best for a few days in the refrigerator wrapped in plastic. Asparagus and herbs should be placed upright in water in the refrigerator.

- To keep celery nice for weeks, wrap it in aluminum foil before putting it in the refrigerator.
- Always store your tomatoes and eggplant on the counter.
- Potatoes and onions should be stored in a cool and dark place but apart from each other.
- Place an apple in the bin with potatoes to keep them from going to seed.
- Winter squash, pumpkin, and whole melons go in a cool vented spot protected from freezing.

What are your tips for a healthy gardener?

ODORS

Remove onion and garlic odors from hands by rubbing fingers with salt moistened with vinegar.

GREASE BURN

When using bacon or hot grease, if it splatters, apply raw honey often on your red spots to prevent them from blistering.

Katie W. Yoder, Goshen, IN

Poison Ivy

Drinking sassafras and burdock tea is good to get rid of poison ivy.

Martha Miller, Edgar, WI

Sore Throat

Red beets can be used for sore throat. Slice the beets and put them on your neck. Wrap a cloth around it to hold the beets in place.

Dianna Yoder, Goshen, IN

SUNBURN

For sunburn relief, use aloe vera gel straight from the plant.

Susie Miller, Dundee, OH

CATNIP TEA

Catnip tea can be grown in your garden. You use this tea before it blooms. Cut off about 5 to 6 stems with leaves; either dry and use later or use it fresh. It may be used as a healthy tea to drink, or it can be used as a soak for any sore muscles or sprains. Soak any part of your body in heated water with the tea leaves. Heat the water again and soak for up to 4 times a day. It also helps with cellulitis; place the tea leaves on that part of your body while you are soaking.

Dianna Yoder, Goshen, IN

CORN SILK TEA

Corn silk from corn stalks is good to make tea with. Drinking it can help with kidney infection and bladder infection.

Dianna Yoder, Goshen, IN

PEAS · BROCOLLI · CARROTS · CAULIFLOWER · SPINACH · CABBAGE · BEETS · POTATOES · ONIONS · APPLES · TURNIPS · LETTUCE · GARLIC · TOMATOES · ZUCCHINI · CUCUMBERS · BEANS · CORN · YAMS · SQUASH · RUTABAGA

RECIPES FOR SALADS

And the earth brought forth grass, and herb yielding seed after his kind, and the tree yielding fruit, whose seed was in itself, after his kind: and God saw that it was good.

GENESIS 1:12

Broccoli Pasta Salad

1 (14 ounce) box ruffled pasta
½ pound bacon
1 (8 ounce) package shredded
  cheddar cheese
½ cup finely chopped fresh
  broccoli

1 onion, grated
2 cups Miracle Whip
¾ cup sugar
3 teaspoons vinegar

Prepare pasta according to package directions; drain and cool. Fry bacon and crumble. Combine pasta, bacon, cheese, broccoli, and onion in large bowl. In small bowl, blend Miracle Whip, sugar, and vinegar. Pour over salad and stir in gently. Optional–add tomatoes and more broccoli.

Joni Miller, Brown City, MI

APPLE SALAD

Apples, chopped or sliced
Nuts, chopped
Celery, chopped
Raisins
Mini marshmallows
1 cup brown sugar

2 teaspoons flour
1 egg, beaten
1 cup water
Vinegar
Pinch salt

Combine apples, nuts, celery, raisins, and mini marshmallows. In saucepan, mix brown sugar, flour, and egg; add water and cook until thick. Add a few drops of vinegar and a pinch of salt. Cool before adding to apple mixture. Stir to coat.

Polly Kuhns, Dunnegan, MO

BROCCOLI-CAULIFLOWER SALAD

1 head broccoli, chopped
1 head cauliflower, chopped
½ pound shredded cheese
1 pound bacon, fried and
   crumbled
1 cup salad dressing or
   mayonnaise

1 cup sour cream
½ cup sugar
½ teaspoon salt
¼ package dry ranch dressing
   mix

Combine broccoli, cauliflower, cheese, and bacon in large bowl. Blend together salad dressing, sour cream, sugar, salt, and ranch mix. Pour over vegetable mixture and stir to coat. Chill.

Viola Beechy, Manawa, WI

Esther Schwartz, Harrisville, PA

GRAPE SALAD

1 cup seedless green grapes, halved
1 large firm banana, sliced
½ cup chopped walnuts
¼ cup blue cheese salad dressing
3 tablespoons mayonnaise
2 teaspoons honey

In small bowl, combine grapes, banana, and walnuts. In another bowl, combine salad dressing, mayonnaise, and honey; pour over grape mixture. Toss to coat. Chill until serving. Yields 2 servings.

Anna Byler, Minerva, OH

LAYERED LETTUCE SALAD

1 head lettuce, cut in small pieces
½ cup chopped celery
½ cup chopped green pepper
1 small can sliced water chestnuts
½ cup chopped onion
1½ cups frozen peas, thawed
2 cups mayonnaise, whipped
2 tablespoons sugar
1 cup shredded cheddar cheese

In 10 x 15-inch pan, layer lettuce, celery, green pepper, chestnuts, onion, and peas in order given. Spread with mayonnaise, then sprinkle with sugar and top with cheese. Cover with plastic and refrigerate for 1 day. Serve at room temperature.

CUCUMBERS WITH CREAM DRESSING

1 cup real mayonnaise
¼ cup sugar
¼ cup vinegar

¼ teaspoon salt
4 cups sliced cucumbers

Blend mayonnaise, sugar, vinegar, and salt. Add cucumbers and toss. Cover and refrigerate for at least 2 hours. Yield: 6 to 8 servings.

FAVORITE CUCUMBER SALAD

2 cups sugar
½ cup vinegar
½ cup water
1 tablespoon salt
1 teaspoon celery seed

8 cups thinly sliced
  cucumbers
1 large onion, chopped
1 medium green pepper,
  chopped

In large bowl, whisk sugar, vinegar, water, salt, and celery seed. Add cucumbers, onion, and pepper. Toss to combine. Refrigerate, covered, at least 1 hour, stirring occasionally.

Esther Peachey, Flemingsburg, KY

Jackson Salad

3 quarts shredded or ground cabbage	1 tablespoon salt
3 onions, chopped	¾ tablespoon mustard seed
3 green peppers, chopped	¾ tablespoon celery seed
1 pint vinegar	½ teaspoon turmeric
	3 cups sugar

Mix cabbage, onions, and peppers in large bowl. In saucepan, bring vinegar, salt, mustard, celery seed, turmeric, and sugar to a boil; cool. Pour dressing over vegetables. Will keep in the refrigerator 3 to 5 days. This is used in many Ohio and Pennsylvania settlements for weddings.

Alma Gingerich, Irvona, PA

POTATO SALAD

12 cups shredded potatoes
12 cups hard-boiled eggs, chopped
½ cup chopped onion
1½ cups chopped celery
3 cups mayonnaise

3 tablespoons vinegar
3 tablespoons mustard
4 teaspoons salt
2 cups sugar
½ cup milk

Cook and shred potatoes. Combine potatoes, eggs, onion, and celery. In separate bowl, mix remaining ingredients, then pour over potato mixture. Mix well and let set overnight.

Betty Bricker, Middlefield, OH

SUMMER SALAD

1 medium cucumber, sliced thin
2 medium yellow summer squash, sliced thin
2 medium tomatoes, sliced
1 sweet onion, sliced
¼ cup vegetable oil

1 teaspoon basil
2 tablespoons lemon juice
2 tablespoons vinegar
1 teaspoon sugar
¼ teaspoon salt
Garlic salt

Arrange cucumbers, squash, tomatoes, and onions on platter. Combine oil, basil, lemon juice, vinegar, sugar, and salt; pour over vegetables. Sprinkle with garlic salt to taste.

Mrs. Freeman Yoder, Millersburg, OH

FRESH VEGETABLE TOSS-UP

1 clove garlic	¼ cup green pepper, cut into strips
1 small head cauliflower	4 carrots, cut into strips
½ head lettuce	½ cup chopped celery
4 tomatoes	1 tablespoon chopped parsley
1 bunch green onion, chopped	French dressing

Halve garlic clove and rub the inside of large salad bowl. Break cauliflower into florets. Tear lettuce into pieces. Mix cauliflower, lettuce, and remaining ingredients except for dressing. When ready to serve, coat with dressing.

Mrs. David C. P. Schwartz, Galesburg, KS

LETTUCE AND EGG SALAD

1 small onion, chopped	⅓ cup milk
½ cup Miracle Whip	8 cups chopped leaf lettuce
⅓ cup sugar	6 hard-boiled eggs, sliced

Blend onion, Miracle Whip, sugar, and milk. When ready to serve, toss with lettuce and eggs.

Emma Miller, Baltic, OH

Becky's Favorite Salad

Dressing:

⅓ cup olive oil
½ cup sugar (can lessen)
2 tablespoons cooking wine
2 tablespoons white or wine vinegar

½ teaspoon salt
¼ teaspoon pepper
½ teaspoon curry powder
1 teaspoon soy sauce

Salad Ingredients:

Romaine lettuce
Baby spinach
Green onion (not too much)
Green apple, chopped

Cashews (could use pecans or walnuts)
Dried cranberries
Feta cheese

Combine dressing ingredients. Best if prepared a day ahead, but it may firm up in refrigerator. Allow to come to room temperature. Pour over salad ingredients.

Sauerkraut Salad

4 cups sauerkraut
1 cup sugar
1 cup shredded carrots

1 cup chopped celery
½ cup chopped onion (or less)

In medium bowl, combine sauerkraut and sugar. Let set for 8 hours. Add carrots, celery, and onion and mix well.

Alice Stauffer, Leonardtown, MD

CORN BREAD SALAD

CORN BREAD:

1 cup milk or buttermilk	1 cup flour
½ cup butter	1 cup cornmeal
½ cup brown sugar	1 teaspoon baking soda
1 egg, beaten	½ teaspoon salt

Combine ingredients and bake in 9 x 13-inch pan at 350 degrees for 30 minutes. Cool.

DRESSING:

1½ cups salad dressing	1½ cups sour cream
1 package Hidden Valley Ranch mix	

Blend together.

SALAD:

1¼ cups or 1 can pinto beans, rinsed and drained	½ cup chopped green pepper
1½ cups corn, drained	1 cup crumbled bacon
¼ cup chopped onion	1 cup shredded cheese
	1 to 2 tomatoes, chopped

Crumble corn bread into 9 x 13-inch pan. Spread dressing on top, then add layer of salad ingredients in order given, topping with tomatoes just before serving. This can be made a day before and refrigerated.

Mrs. Paul Schrock, Salem, MO

Recipes for Soups

*There is nothing better for a man, than that he should
eat and drink, and that he should make his soul
enjoy good in his labour. This also I saw,
that it was from the hand of God.*

Ecclesiastes 2:24

Butternut Squash Soup

2 tablespoons butter
5 cups cubed, peeled winter
  squash (like butternut)
2 cups cubed, peeled potatoes
1 teaspoon salt

½ teaspoon pepper
2 cups diced onion
4 cups chicken broth
1 cup heavy cream

In large pot, melt butter over medium heat. Add squash, potatoes, salt, pepper, and onion. Stir and cook 3 to 4 minutes. Stir in broth. Reduce heat and simmer 20 minutes or until vegetables are tender, stirring occasionally. Blend soup mixture until smooth. Stir in cream and serve.

Anna Zook, Dalton, OH

Asparagus Soup

1 small onion, chopped
1 stalk celery, chopped
Butter
4 cups chicken broth

1 pound asparagus
1 potato, peeled and chopped
3 tablespoons flour
Salt and pepper

In large pot, lightly sauté onion and celery in butter. Add 3 cups broth, asparagus, and potato and cook until softened. Allow to cool, and blend until smooth. Return to heat. Combine 1 cup broth and flour into a paste. Slowly add to near-boiling soup and stir until thickened. Season to taste with salt and pepper. Optional: Serve garnished with bacon crumbles, goat cheese, and/or sour cream.

Cazuela de Elsa Soup

2 medium carrots, peeled and
  sliced
1 medium yellow onion,
  chopped
1 medium sweet potato,
  peeled and cubed
3 pounds chicken, cubed
6 medium cloves garlic,
  minced

4 teaspoons salt
5 cups water
1 large green pepper, cored
  and sliced
1 medium tomato, chopped
2 ears of corn, sliced from
  cob
¼ cup cilantro, chopped
Pepper, to taste

Prepare all vegetables. In tall narrow stockpot, bring carrots, onion, sweet potato, chicken, garlic, and salt to a boil in water. Lower heat and simmer for 15 minutes. Add green pepper, tomato, and corn. Cover; bring to a boil; lower heat and simmer partially covered for 5 minutes. Stir in cilantro and pepper. Simmer additional 2 minutes. Yields: 13 cups.

Barbara Beechy, Manawa, WI

CHEESEBURGER SOUP

4 pounds hamburger
1½ cups chopped onion
2 cups chicken broth
4 cups water
3 cups chopped celery
3 cups chopped carrots
9 cups chopped potatoes
3 teaspoons salt
1½ teaspoons pepper

1 cup butter
1¾ cups flour
6 cups milk
6 cups Velveeta cheese
1 teaspoon onion salt (optional)
1 teaspoon Greek seasoning
½ teaspoon garlic salt (optional)

Fry hamburger and onion; drain. In 12-quart pot, bring broth, water, celery, carrots, potatoes, salt, and pepper to a boil. In saucepan, melt butter and stir in flour, then slowly stir in milk; cook until thick. Add cheese; stir until melted. Add optional seasonings to taste. When vegetables have cooked to soft texture, pour sauce into boiling vegetables. Stir in hamburger mixture. This soup is a good one to freeze for future meals.

Mrs. Kenneth A. Schrock, Monroe, WI

CHICKEN VEGETABLE SOUP

1 to 2 chickens
4 cups green beans
3 cups chopped carrots
¾ cup chopped green pepper
2 cups chopped celery
1 cup chopped onion
5 cups corn

6 cups chopped potatoes
2 cups tomato chunks
Salt
Parsley
Red pepper flakes
1½ cups dried spaghetti

Cook chicken in broth, debone, and add back to broth. Bring to a boil. Add vegetables one at a time, bringing broth to a boil between each addition. Add salt, parsley, and pepper flakes to taste. Add spaghetti and cook 10 minutes before serving. This is a good soup to take to work in a thermos on a winter day.

Joni Miller, Brown City, MI

SUMMER GARDEN CHILI

1 pound hamburger
2 medium onions, chopped
2 large green peppers,
  chopped
4 cloves garlic, minced
2 tablespoons oil
½ teaspoon cumin

2 tablespoons chili powder
1 teaspoon oregano
¾ teaspoon salt
2 cans kidney beans
4 large tomatoes, chunked, or
  1 quart canned tomatoes
2 cups water (eliminate if
  using canned tomatoes)

Brown hamburger in dutch oven. Remove and wipe out grease. Sauté onion, pepper, and garlic in oil over medium heat until soft, about 5 minutes. Add cumin, chili powder, oregano, and salt. Cook 1 minute. Add beans, tomatoes, and water (if using). Bring to a boil, reduce heat, and simmer 30 minutes.

Susie Miller, Dundee, OH

Pizza Soup

1 pound hamburger	1 cup dried pasta
½ cup chopped onion	4 cups pizza sauce
¼ cup chopped green pepper	4 to 6 ounces mushrooms
2 cups water	1 to 3 ounces pepperoni,
2 teaspoons salt	diced
1 cup diced carrots	1 cup peas
1 cup diced potatoes	Cheese
	4 tablespoons butter

In large pot, brown hamburger with onion and green pepper. Add water, salt, carrots, and potatoes. Cook 5 to 10 minutes, then add pasta, pizza sauce, mushrooms, pepperoni, peas, and cheese to your taste. Simmer 30 minutes. Add butter and serve.

Lorene Helmuth, Junction City, WI

Sausage, Greens, and Potato Soup

1 pound sausage	2 pounds potatoes, peeled
1 tablespoon oil	and chopped
3 cloves garlic, minced	Salt and pepper
1 medium onion, chopped	1 cup heavy whipping cream
4 cups chicken broth	2 cups chopped greens
2 cups water	(spinach, kale, lamb's-quarter, chard, or dandelion)

In pot, cook sausage in oil. When half done, add garlic and onion; cook until browned. Add broth, water, potatoes, and salt and pepper to taste; cook until potatoes are tender. Add cream and greens. Cook until tender and wilted.

Lizzie's Favorite Soup

3 cups chopped potatoes and/
  or broccoli
½ cup sliced celery
½ cup sliced carrots
¼ cup chopped onion
1 cup water
1 teaspoon parsley flakes
1 chicken bouillon cube or 1
  teaspoon chicken base
½ teaspoon salt
⅛ teaspoon pepper
1 teaspoon Mrs. Dash
  Original Blend (optional)
2 tablespoons flour
1½ cups milk
1 pound browned sausage
½ pound Velveeta cheese,
  cubed

In 3-quart saucepan, mix vegetables, water, parsley, bouillon, salt, pepper, and Mrs. Dash Original Blend, if desired. Simmer for 15 to 20 minutes or until vegetables are tender. Mix flour with milk and add to simmering vegetables. Cook until thickened. Reduce heat and add sausage and cheese. Stir until melted. For a thinner soup, add more milk.

Lizzie Hershberger, Navarre, OH

Cheesy Potato Soup

½ cup chopped carrots
1½ cups chopped celery
1 cup chopped onion
4½ cups chopped potatoes
2 cans cream of chicken soup
2 cups water
½ pound Velveeta cheese
Salt and pepper

Boil vegetables in 2 quarts of water for 20 minutes. Add cream of chicken soup, water, and Velveeta cheese. Season with salt and pepper to taste.

Katie W. Yoder, Goshen, IN

Spaghetti Soup

3 celery stalks, chopped
4 carrots, chopped
½ onion, chopped
1¼ pounds hamburger,
    cooked and drained
1 quart tomato juice
¼ teaspoon marjoram

1 teaspoon parsley flakes
1 teaspoon basil
⅛ teaspoon garlic powder
½ teaspoon Italian seasoning
1 tablespoon brown sugar
3 ounces dried spaghetti

Cover vegetables with water, cover, and cook 10 minutes. Add remaining ingredients except for spaghetti, and simmer until vegetables are tender. Break spaghetti into small pieces and cook in water until just tender; drain. Add to soup just before serving. If soup is too strong, add water. The longer it cooks, the better. This soup will freeze well.

Esther Schlabach, Vanleer, TN

CREAMY TURKEY VEGETABLE SOUP

1 cup diced carrots
½ cup diced celery
⅓ cup chopped onion
2 tablespoons butter
2 cups diced cooked turkey
2 cups water

1½ cups peeled, diced potatoes
2 teaspoons chicken bouillon granules
½ teaspoon salt
½ teaspoon pepper
2½ cups milk
3 tablespoons flour

In large saucepan, sauté carrots, celery, and onion in butter until tender. Add turkey, water, potatoes, bouillon, salt, and pepper. Bring to a boil. Reduce heat, cover, and simmer for 10 to 12 minutes or until vegetables are tender. Stir in 2 cups milk. In separate bowl, combine flour with remaining ½ cup milk; blend until smooth. Stir into soup. Bring to a boil; cook and stir for 2 minutes or until thickened.

Edna Irene Miller, Arthur, IL

CREAMY ZUCCHINI SOUP

2 tablespoons diced onion
3 tablespoons butter
3 tablespoons flour
2 cups milk
1 cup water

1 teaspoon chicken base
¾ teaspoon salt
¼ teaspoon pepper
1 large zucchini, shredded
1 cup shredded cheddar cheese

Brown onion in butter until tender. Stir in flour; gradually add milk and water. Season with chicken base, salt, and pepper. Bring to a boil. Cook and stir for 2 minutes. Add zucchini; cook until tender. Stir in cheese until melted.

Clara Beachy, Campbell Hill, IL

Recipes for Main Dishes

He did good, and gave us rain from heaven,
and fruitful seasons, filling our hearts
with food and gladness.

Acts 14:17

Garden Skillet

2 pounds ground bulk
  sausage
5 medium red potatoes,
  sliced
4 medium carrots, sliced
3 medium zucchini, sliced
4 cups cut green beans

1 medium onion, chopped
1 medium tomato, cut into
  wedges
1 red or green pepper,
  chopped
1 teaspoon Accent
Salt and pepper, to taste

In large skillet, fry sausage until no longer pink. Add potatoes and carrots; cook 5 minutes. Then add remaining vegetables and seasoning. Steam until all are tender.

Rebecca T. Christner, Bryant, IN

SUMMER STIR-FRY

2 tablespoons butter
1 cup shredded zucchini
Leftover boiled or fried
   potatoes
Chopped onion

6 eggs, beaten
Cheese, shredded
Tomatoes, chopped
Green peppers, chopped

Melt butter in a large frying pan; add zucchini, potatoes, and onion. Cook until onion is tender. Add beaten eggs; scramble. When eggs are cooked, top with cheese. Serve with topping of tomatoes and green pepper.

Mary Grace Peachey, Catlett, VA

POTATO HAYSTACK CASSEROLE

8 to 10 medium potatoes
1 cup ranch dressing
1 cup milk
2 pounds hamburger
Onion
2 packages dry taco
   seasoning

¼ cup butter
½ cup flour
3 cups milk
3 cups shredded cheese
Crushed nacho chips

Cook and dice potatoes. Put in bottom of roaster. Mix dressing and milk; pour over potatoes. Brown hamburger with some onion and taco seasoning. Put on top of potatoes. Combine butter with flour and cook until golden. Slowly add milk, stirring until thickened. Stir in cheese until melted. Pour cheese sauce over meat layer. Bake at 325 degrees for about 1 hour, until heated through. Crush chips on top before serving.

Katie Zook, Apple Creek, OH

SIX-LAYER DINNER

Bacon slices	Salt
1 to 1½ pounds hamburger, browned	Peas
6 medium potatoes, sliced	Carrots
1 to 2 onions, sliced	Mushrooms
	Shredded cheese

In 6-quart kettle, line bottom with bacon topped with hamburger. Add layers of potatoes and onion. Sprinkle with salt. Add your choice of vegetables. Start burner on high to fry bacon at bottom of pot. Lower heat, cover, and cook until potatoes and vegetables are tender when pierced by a fork. Do not stir. Top with cheese. Delicious and easy!

Mrs. Paul Schrock, Salem, MO

POTATO HAYSTACK

8 to 10 pounds potatoes	Salt and pepper, to taste
2 packages dry ranch dressing mix	4 pounds hamburger
2 cups sour cream	Onion
2 cups milk	1 or 2 packages dry taco seasoning
2 cans cream of mushroom soup	Shredded cheese
	Doritos chips

Cook and shred potatoes. Mix ranch dressing, sour cream, milk, mushroom soup, salt, and pepper together; add to potatoes. Fry hamburger with some onion and taco seasoning to your taste. Layer meat in casserole dish with potatoes and cheese. Bake at 350 degrees for 1 hour. Crush Doritos on top before serving.

Variation: Omit the mushroom soup and cheese and substitute homemade or canned cheese sauce. Pour over the layers of meat and potatoes before baking.

Verena Schwartz, Scottsburg, IN

CHICKEN AND BISCUIT CASSEROLE

1 quart chicken broth
1 tablespoon chicken
  seasoning
1 cup chopped potatoes
1 cup chopped celery

1 cup chopped carrots
1 cup peas (optional)
1 cup cooked chicken
4 tablespoons flour

In pot, blend broth and seasoning; cook potatoes, celery, carrots, and peas until tender. Blend flour with a bit of water to make a paste. Stir into boiling vegetable mixture. Put into 9 x 13-inch pan and top with biscuits.

BISCUITS:

2 cups flour
2 teaspoons baking powder
½ teaspoon cream of tartar
½ teaspoon salt

2 tablespoons sugar
½ cup shortening
⅔ cup milk
1 egg, beaten

Mix dry ingredients together. Cut in shortening until crumbly. Combine milk and egg. Stir into other mixture until crumbs are just moistened. Pat together and place on flat surface; roll and cut.

Bake at 350 degrees for 30 to 35 minutes until biscuits are done.

Mrs. John Miller, Remus, MI

Taco Stuffed Peppers

4 bell peppers, cut in half and
  cored
1 pound hamburger
1 package taco seasoning
¼ cup water

1 cup salsa
8 ounces canned red kidney
  beans, drained
Cheddar cheese

Put peppers in boiling water for 3 minutes. Fry hamburger. Add taco
seasoning, water, salsa, and kidney beans; simmer for 5 minutes. Place
peppers in oven-safe pan with lid. Put mixture in peppers, cover, and put
in oven at 350 degrees for 20 minutes. Remove from oven and top with
cheddar cheese, then return to oven until cheese melts. Serve with sour
cream and tomatoes.

Ruth Yoder, Goshen, IN

Spaghetti Corn

1 cup dried spaghetti, broken
2 to 4 cups corn
1 cup milk

2 cups cooked meat
  (hamburger, ham, chicken)
1 cup grated cheese
Salt and pepper, to taste

Mix all ingredients in casserole dish, cover, and bake at 350 degrees for 1 hour.

Mrs. Peter Landis, Brodhead, WI

Chicken in a Crumb Basket

Crumb Basket:

½ cup melted butter
6 cups bread crumbs
¼ cup chopped onion

1 teaspoon celery salt
½ teaspoon poultry seasoning

Mix all ingredients together and line bottom and sides of casserole dish, forming a "basket." Bake at 350 degrees for 15 minutes.

Filling:

¼ cup butter
¼ cup flour
½ cup milk
1½ cups chicken broth

1 cup finely chopped carrots
1 cup finely chopped potatoes
3 cups finely chopped cooked
  chicken
1 cup peas

Make white sauce by melting butter, browning flour in butter, then slowly adding milk then broth. In separate pot, cook carrots and potatoes in water until soft; drain. Add chicken and peas; coat with white sauce. Pour into crumb basket and bake at 350 degrees for 30 to 40 minutes.

Susan Byler, Crab Orchard, KY

FROGMORE STEW

1 cup ketchup
1 cup cooking oil
1 cup apple cider vinegar
¾ cup salt
1 teaspoon pepper
1 (3 ounce) package crab boil
  seasoning mix
14 small red potatoes, left
  whole and unpeeled
1 pound baby carrots, left
  whole
18 half ears corn

5 pounds chicken breast, cut
  into pieces
4 pounds smoked sausage,
  cut into pieces
2 (8 ounce) packages fresh
  mushrooms
2 cups chopped onion
2 pounds medium shrimp,
  cleaned
Barbecue sauce
Shrimp cocktail sauce
Sour cream
Melted butter

Mix first 5 ingredients in large 20-quart kettle, fill ⅓ full with water, and bring to a boil. Mix in crab seasoning. Add potatoes and carrots and return to a hard boil for 5 to 10 minutes. Add corn and chicken; boil for 5 minutes. Add sausage, mushrooms, and onion; boil for 5 minutes. Add shrimp. Make sure broth keeps boiling through each addition. Remove from heat and let stand at least 5 minutes while you prepare the table.

Cover table with clean vinyl or plastic cloth. Run strip of foil down center of table. Drain broth from stew; dump stew onto foil down the length of the table so everyone will be able to reach some. Pass around bowls of barbecue sauce, shrimp cocktail sauce, sour cream, and melted butter so that everyone can put a dollop of whatever sauces they want on the table in front of them to dip their stew in. Eat with your fingers and enjoy! Recipe feeds 8 to 10 people.

Mary Gingerich, Kimbolton, OH

Stuffed Pepper Casserole

2 pounds hamburger,
    browned
1½ cups chopped cabbage
1 large tomato, peeled and
    chopped
2 large yellow tomatoes,
    peeled and chopped
1¼ cups uncooked instant rice

1 medium onion, chopped
2 red peppers, chopped
2 green peppers, chopped
2½ cups water
1 tablespoon salt (or to taste)
1 teaspoon pepper
1 cup shredded cheddar
    cheese

Combine all ingredients except cheese. Pour into baking dish with lid.
Top with cheese. Bake covered at 375 degrees for 1½ hours or until rice is
tender.

Lucy Zimmerman, Orrstown, PA

Easy Veggie Quiche

Vegetables (zucchini, tomatoes, sweet onion), cubed
1 teaspoon salt
Oregano, basil, and garlic salt, to taste

2 pounds hamburger, browned and drained
½ cup mayonnaise
½ cup yogurt
1 cup milk
6 eggs, beaten
Shredded cheese

Layer vegetables in 9 x 13-inch pan. Sprinkle with salt and herbs. Top with hamburger. Mix mayonnaise, yogurt, milk, and eggs together; pour over layered hamburger and vegetables. Bake uncovered at 350 degrees for 1 hour and 15 minutes. Top with cheese during last 10 minutes.

Christina Peight, Belleville, PA

Tex-Mex Summer Squash Casserole

7 medium yellow squash or zucchini, sliced (about 10 cups)

2¼ cups shredded cheddar cheese, divided

1 medium red onion, chopped

1 (4 ounce) can chopped green chiles

1 small can diced jalapeño peppers, drained

¼ cup flour

½ teaspoon salt

¾ cup salsa

4 green onions, sliced

¼ cup chopped red onion

In large bowl, combine squash, ¾ cup cheese, red onion, chiles, and jalapeños. Sprinkle with flour and salt; toss gently to combine. Transfer to greased 9 x 13-inch baking dish. Bake covered at 400 degrees for 30 to 40 minutes or until squash is tender. Spoon salsa over top, sprinkle with remaining cheese. Bake uncovered for 10 to 15 minutes or until golden brown. Let stand 10 minutes. Top with green onions and ¼ cup chopped red onion. Yield: 10 servings.

Mary Yoder, Millersburg, OH

Ida's Good Stew

Cabbage leaves

Chopped cabbage

Carrots

Green beans

Potatoes

2 packages brats or other meat

Salt and pepper

Put cabbage leaves on bottom of casserole dish. Cut up cabbage, carrots, green beans, and potatoes into bite-size pieces. Cut brats into quarters. Season to taste with salt and pepper. Bake at 350 degrees for 1½ hours in oven or on high in slow cooker.

Ida Hochstetler, Shipshewana, IN

Deluxe Zucchini Casserole

2 cups zucchini and/or yellow squash, cubed and cooked
2 pounds sausage
1 can cream of mushroom soup
1 cup Ritz cracker crumbs
1 cup shredded cheese
⅓ cup chopped onion
2 eggs, beaten
Salt, to taste
Pepper, to taste
Italian seasoning, to taste
Garlic salt, to taste

Combine all and put into greased 9 x 13-inch pan.

Topping:

¼ cup butter, melted
1 cup shredded cheese
1 cup Ritz cracker crumbs
Parmesan cheese

Combine butter with cheese and cracker crumbs. Spread over zucchini mixture. Sprinkle with Parmesan cheese. Bake at 350 degrees for 45 minutes.

Try using hamburger instead of sausage and replace Italian seasoning with taco seasoning mix.

Mary Mast, Hamptonville, NC

Grandma's Cabbage

1 pound sausage
½ head cabbage, shredded
Seasoned salt

Brown sausage; add cabbage and brown lightly. Season to taste with seasoned salt. Cover and steam cabbage for 15 minutes. To serve, drizzle with ranch or your favorite dressing.

Luella Miller, Shreve, OH

Upside-Down Dinner Casserole

½ pound bacon	2 tablespoons flour
1½ pounds hamburger	5 or 6 potatoes, sliced
2 medium onions, sliced	Salt and pepper
1 pound carrots, sliced	White sauce (recipe below)

Cover bottom of casserole dish with bacon slices. Press hamburger on top of bacon. Follow with layers of onions and carrots. Season with salt. Sift flour over carrots. Layer on potatoes. Season with salt and pepper. Cover with white sauce. Cover and bake at 375 degrees for 1½ hours, until vegetables are tender.

White Sauce:

4 tablespoons butter	1 teaspoon parsley flakes
4 tablespoons flour	1 teaspoon diced chives
1 teaspoon salt	1¼ cups milk
¼ teaspoon pepper	

Melt butter in saucepan. Add flour, salt, pepper, parsley, and chives; stir until well blended. Cook for 2 minutes, stirring constantly. Gradually add milk; continue stirring until all milk is incorporated and sauce thickens. Remove from heat.

Edna Irene Miller, Arthur, IL

Sausage Stuffed Zucchini

4 medium (6- to 7-inch)
zucchini
½ pound bulk sausage
¼ cup chopped onion
1 clove garlic, minced

1 teaspoon oregano
½ cup fresh or frozen corn
1 medium tomato, diced
1 cup shredded cheddar
cheese, divided

Cut zucchini in half lengthwise. Place cut side down in large skillet with ½ inch water. Bring to a boil, reduce heat, and simmer until zucchini are crisp yet tender–about 5 minutes. Remove and drain water. Sauté sausage, onion, and garlic until browned, drain. Add oregano, corn, and tomato; cook and stir until heated through. Remove from heat and stir in ⅔ cup cheese; set aside. Scoop out and discard seeds from zucchini. Divide sausage mixture among zucchini shells. Place in greased 9 x 13-inch baking pan. Sprinkle with remaining cheese. Bake uncovered at 375 degrees for 12 to 15 minutes, or until heated through.

Mary Yoder, Millersburg, OH

HOT VEGETABLE PIZZA

CRUST:

2 tablespoons yeast
2 teaspoons sugar
⅔ cup warm water
2 cups cold water
2 tablespoons sugar

3 tablespoons oil
1 teaspoon salt
6½ cups flour, divided
¼ cup oil

In small bowl, combine yeast, 2 teaspoons sugar, and warm water; stir to dissolve. Set aside. In large bowl, mix cold water, 2 tablespoons sugar, 3 tablespoons oil, 3 cups flour, and salt; beat until smooth. Add in yeast mixture, which should appear bubbly. Add 3½ cups flour and work until elasticized. Let rise until doubled in size. Put ¼ cup oil on a large cookie sheet, then press dough over it. Let rise 5 to 10 minutes before baking at 400 degrees for 10 to 15 minutes.

TOPPING:

1½ to 2 cups each of your
choice of vegetables
(potatoes, carrots, broccoli,
cauliflower, etc.)

2 cups chopped ham

Bring vegetables to a boil in a little water; cook until soft; drain. Spread vegetables and ham over pizza crust.

SAUCE:

2 tablespoons lard
1 cup flour
2 to 4 cups milk

Cheese powder
Velveeta cheese
Salt and pepper, to taste

Melt lard in 3-quart pan, stir in flour and brown. Add milk slowly and cook until thickened, stirring constantly with a whisk. Add cheese powder and Velveeta cheese to taste. Season with salt and pepper. Pour over vegetables. Allow to settle before cutting to serve.

Mrs. Samuel J. Schwartz, Bryant, IN

SANTA FE CORNMEAL PIZZA (GLUTEN FREE)

CRUST:

1 cup cornmeal

1⅓ cups water, divided

2 tablespoons Parmesan cheese

In small bowl, combine cornmeal and ⅔ cup water. In saucepan, bring remaining water to a boil. Gradually add cornmeal mixture; cook and stir until thickened. Stir in cheese. When cool enough to handle, pat into greased 12-inch pan. Bake at 375 degrees for 15 minutes or until golden brown. Top with your choice of toppings or follow recipe below.

1 medium onion, chopped

1 green pepper, julienned

1 clove garlic, minced

1 tablespoon olive oil

1 (8 ounce) can tomato sauce

8 fresh mushrooms, sliced

¾ teaspoon basil

¾ teaspoon oregano

¼ teaspoon pepper

2 cups cooked black beans

1½ cups shredded mozzarella cheese, divided

4 tablespoons Parmesan cheese, divided

½ cup sliced black olives

Sauté onion, green pepper, and garlic in oil until tender. Add tomato sauce, mushrooms, basil, oregano, and pepper; cover and cook 5 minutes. Add beans. Sprinkle ½ cup mozzarella cheese and 2 tablespoons Parmesan cheese onto the cornmeal crust. Top with bean mixture and remaining cheeses. Sprinkle with olives. Bake at 375 degrees for 10 to 15 minutes or until cheese melts.

Phebe Peight, McVeytown, PA

Fresh Tomato Pizza with Herbed Crust

1 tablespoon honey	Tomatoes
1 tablespoon yeast	Salt
1 cup warm water	Pepper
1 tablespoon basil	Olives
1 tablespoon oregano	Green peppers
½ tablespoon garlic powder	Onions
2¼ to 2½ cups whole wheat flour	Fresh basil
Olive oil	Cheese

Mix honey, yeast, and water. Let stand until bubbly. Mix in basil, oregano, and garlic; add flour gradually until smooth. Knead along with a few drops of olive oil. Spread onto pizza pan and let rise. Bake at 400 degrees for 8 minutes. Layer thinly sliced tomatoes on crust, slightly overlapping. Drizzle with olive oil. Top with salt, pepper, olives, green peppers, onions, basil, and cheese. Bake about 10 minutes until cheese is melted and crust lightly browned.

Phebe Peight, McVeytown, PA

HOBOS

Cabbage
Hamburger patties
Shredded potatoes
Salt and pepper

Sliced onions
Cream of mushroom soup
Velveeta cheese
Shredded carrots

Lay a large piece of foil on counter. Try to break off largest piece of cabbage leaf you can and set it in middle of foil. Place good thick "seasoned to your liking" hamburger patty on top. Now add layer of shredded potatoes; season with salt and pepper. Can't go without onions, so add those. Next, add dollop of cream of mushroom soup. Place good thick slice of Velveeta cheese on top. Oh, and put some shredded carrots on now. Roll and fold foil tightly so that it won't come undone while grilling. Make one foil packet per person. Place packets on grill on low heat for 1 hour or until done. This is an all-in-one meal.

Mary Alice Yoder, Topeka, IN

Camp More

4 cups red potatoes,
  quartered
2 green peppers, cut into
  ½-inch slices
2 banana peppers, cut into
  ½-inch rings

1 large onion, cut into 1-inch
  chunks
1 package Lit'l Smokies
  sausages
¼ cup butter
Salt, to taste

Combine all but salt and fry in cast-iron skillet over campfire. Season with salt when almost done.

Mrs. Samuel Gingerich, Danville, OH

Porky Pie

4 medium sweet potatoes,
  peeled and cubed
2 tablespoons butter
1½ teaspoons sugar
1½ teaspoons salt
½ teaspoon cinnamon

Milk
1 pound ground pork
2 tablespoons flour
Dash pepper
1½ cups water

Cook potatoes in salted water until tender; drain. Mash slightly; add butter, sugar, salt, and cinnamon. If necessary, add a little milk to help it combine. Brown pork in skillet; drain, reserving grease. In skillet, add flour and pepper to grease; slowly stir in water to make gravy. Cook until it starts to thicken. Cover bottom of shallow baking dish with cooked pork; pour gravy over pork. Spread sweet potato mixture over top. Bake at 400 degrees for 20 minutes.

Mary Grace Peachey, Catlett, VA

PEAS · BROCOLLI · CARROTS · CAULIFLOWER · SPINACH · CABBAGE · BEETS · POTA
uliflower · spinach · cabbage · beets · potatoes · onions · apples · turnips · lettuce
SH · RUTABAGA · PEAS · BROCOLLI · CARROTS · CAULIFLOWER · SPINACH · CABBAG
spinach · cabbage · beets · potatoes · onions · apples · turnips · lettuce · garlic · toma
N · YAMS · SQUASH · RUTABAGA · PEAS · BROCOLLI · CARROTS · CAULIFLOWER · SPI
bage · beets · potatoes · onions · apples · turnips · lettuce · garlic · tomatoes · zucchini
BEANS · CORN · YAMS · SQUASH · RUTABAGA · PEAS · BROCOLLI · CARROTS
toes · onions · apples · turnips · lettuce · garlic · tomatoes · zucchini · cucumbers · bear
UCCHINI · CUCUMBERS · BEANS · CORN · YAMS · SQUASH · RUTABAGA · PEAS · B
ples · turnips · lettuce · garlic · tomatoes · zucchini · cucumbers · beans · corn · yams
RLIC · TOMATOES · ZUCCHINI · CUCUMBERS · BEANS · CORN · YAMS · SQUASH · R
ettuce · garlic · tomatoes · zucchini · cucumbers · beans · corn · yams · squash · rutabag
NIPS · LETTUCE · GARLIC · TOMATOES · ZUCCHINI · CUCUMBERS · BEANS · CORN
atoes · zucchini · cucumbers · beans · corn · yams · squash · rutabaga · peas · brocolli
IONS · APPLES · TURNIPS · LETTUCE · GARLIC · TOMATOES · ZUCCHINI · CUCUMB
cucumbers · beans · corn · yams · squash · rutabaga · peas · brocolli · carrots · cauli
TS · POTATOES · ONIONS · APPLES · TURNIPS · LETTUCE · GARLIC · TOMATOES · ZUC
beans · corn · yams · squash · rutabaga · peas · brocolli · carrots · cauliflower · spir
ABBAGE · BEETS · POTATOES · ONIONS · APPLES · TURNIPS · LETTUCE · GARLIC · TO
yams · squash · rutabaga · peas · brocolli · carrots · cauliflower · spinach · cabbage
R · SPINACH · CABBAGE · BEETS · POTATOES · ONIONS · APPLES · TURNIPS · LETT
sh · rutabaga · peas · brocolli · carrots · cauliflower · spinach · cabbage · beets · potate
RROTS · CAULIFLOWER · SPINACH · CABBAGE · BEETS · POTATOES · ONIONS · APP
peas · brocolli · carrots · cauliflower · spinach · cabbage · beets · potatoes · onions · o
EAS · BROCOLLI · CARROTS · CAULIFLOWER · SPINACH · CABBAGE · BEETS · POTATO
lli · carrots · cauliflower · spinach · cabbage · beets · potatoes · onions · apples · turnip
H · RUTABAGA · PEAS · BROCOLLI · CARROTS · CAULIFLOWER · SPINACH · CABBAG
auliflower · spinach · cabbage · beets · potatoes · onions · apples · turnips · lettuce
N · YAMS · SQUASH · RUTABAGA · PEAS · BROCOLLI · CARROTS · CAULIFLOWER · SPI
spinach · cabbage · beets · potatoes · onions · apples · turnips · lettuce · garlic · toma
BEANS · CORN · YAMS · SQUASH · RUTABAGA · PEAS · BROCOLLI · CARROTS
bbage · beets · potatoes · onions · apples · turnips · lettuce · garlic · tomatoes · zucchini
UCCHINI · CUCUMBERS · BEANS · CORN · YAMS · SQUASH · RUTABAGA · PEAS · B
atoes · onions · apples · turnips · lettuce · garlic · tomatoes · zucchini · cucumbers · bear
RLIC · TOMATOES · ZUCCHINI · CUCUMBERS · BEANS · CORN · YAMS · SQUASH · R
ples · turnips · lettuce · garlic · tomatoes · zucchini · cucumbers · beans · corn · yams
NIPS · LETTUCE · GARLIC · TOMATOES · ZUCCHINI · CUCUMBERS · BEANS · CORN
ettuce · garlic · tomatoes · zucchini · cucumbers · beans · corn · yams · squash · rutabag
IONS · APPLES · TURNIPS · LETTUCE · GARLIC · TOMATOES · ZUCCHINI · CUCUMB
natoes · zucchini · cucumbers · beans · corn · yams · squash · rutabaga · peas · brocolli
TS · POTATOES · ONIONS · APPLES · TURNIPS · LETTUCE · GARLIC · TOMATOES · ZUC
cucumbers · beans · corn · yams · squash · rutabaga · peas · brocolli · carrots · cauli
ABBAGE · BEETS · POTATOES · ONIONS · APPLES · TURNIPS · LETTUCE · GARLIC · TO
beans · corn · yams · squash · rutabaga · peas · brocolli · carrots · cauliflower · spir
R · SPINACH · CABBAGE · BEETS · POTATOES · ONIONS · APPLES · TURNIPS · LETT
yams · squash · rutabaga · peas · brocolli · carrots · cauliflower · spinach · cabbage
RROTS · CAULIFLOWER · SPINACH · CABBAGE · BEETS · POTATOES · ONIONS · APP
sh · rutabaga · peas · brocolli · carrots · cauliflower · spinach · cabbage · beets · potat
EAS · BROCOLLI · CARROTS · CAULIFLOWER · SPINACH · CABBAGE · BEETS · POTATO
peas · brocolli · carrots · cauliflower · spinach · cabbage · beets · potatoes · onions
H · RUTABAGA · PEAS · BROCOLLI · CARROTS · CAULIFLOWER · SPINACH · CABBAG
lli · carrots · cauliflower · spinach · cabbage · beets · potatoes · onions · apples · turnips
· YAMS · SQUASH · RUTABAGA · PEAS · BROCOLLI · CARROTS · CAULIFLOWER · SPI

Recipes for Sides

For the earth bringeth forth fruit of herself; first the blade,
then the ear, after that the full corn in the ear.

Mark 4:28

Cold Vegetable Pizza

2 cups flour
3 teaspoons baking powder
1 teaspoon salt
6 tablespoons shortening
⅔ cup milk

1 (8 ounce) package cream cheese
Ranch dressing
Fresh chopped vegetables (tomatoes, peppers, lettuce, carrots, etc.)
Shredded cheese

Mix flour, baking powder, salt, shortening, and milk into dough. Spread onto lightly greased baking sheet. Bake at 350 degrees for 10 to 15 minutes, until lightly browned. Cool. Combine cream cheese with enough ranch dressing to make spread; smooth over cooled crust. Top with vegetables and cheese. Drizzle a little ranch dressing over pizza. Chill.

Rebecca Schwartz, Bryant, IN

Pickled Eggs and Red Beets

2 tablespoons plus 1 teaspoon vinegar
Water
½ cup sugar
1 teaspoon salt

Dash pepper
1 can sliced beets
1 dozen eggs, hard-boiled and peeled

Pour vinegar in measuring cup and fill to the ¾-cup line with water. In bowl, mix vinegar-water mixture with sugar, salt, and pepper; add beets. Place eggs in large jar; pour beets and juice over them. Chill at least 12 hours.

Mary H. Miller, Heuvelton, NY

Roasted Vegetables

Pick any fresh vegetables of your choice. We enjoy potatoes, green beans, peppers, onions, zucchini, carrots, cauliflower, and mushrooms. The key to roasting different types of vegetables at the same time is to cut hard vegetables, like carrots and potatoes, into smaller pieces than the softer vegetables. Coat veggies with a little Italian dressing, olive oil, or butter, then sprinkle with your choice of herbs and seasonings. Toss together until coated. Spread in single layer on baking sheet. Bake at 425 to 450 degrees until tender and nicely roasted. Stir at least once.

Phebe Peight, McVeytown, PA

SCALLOPED ASPARAGUS

4 cups chopped fresh
  asparagus
1½ cups milk
2 tablespoons flour
1 teaspoon salt

½ teaspoon pepper
½ cup grated cheese
1 cup bread crumbs, divided
2 tablespoons butter, cubed

Cook asparagus in a little water until tender. Place in buttered baking dish. Combine milk, flour, salt, and pepper; pour over asparagus. Top with cheese and ½ cup bread crumbs; stir into asparagus mixture. Dot with cubed butter; sprinkle with remaining bread crumbs. Bake at 325 degrees for 30 minutes or until browned.

Laura Brenneman, Stanwood, MI

CALIFORNIA BLEND CASSEROLE

2½ pounds California blend vegetables (large chopped pieces of cauliflower, broccoli, and carrots)
1 (10.75 ounce) can cream of mushroom soup
1 teaspoon salt
½ teaspoon pepper
½ pound Velveeta cheese, chopped
½ cup melted butter
2 cups crushed Ritz crackers

Cook vegetables in a little water for 10 minutes; drain and put into 9 x 13-inch pan. Combine soup, salt, pepper, and cheese; pour over vegetables. Mix butter and crackers; spread over top of vegetables. Bake at 350 degrees for 1 hour.

Susan Yoder, Montezuma, GA

CREAMED CABBAGE

1 head cabbage
1 small onion
Salt
Sugar
½ cup butter
½ cup flour
1 cup cream

Cut cabbage in ¼-inch thick slices. Place in saucepan with sliced onion. Sprinkle salt and sugar to taste. Add just enough water to cover, and bring to a boil. Turn off heat; let sit covered. In separate saucepan, melt butter and blend in flour. Use some cabbage water to thin it a bit. Spoon in drained cabbage. Stir in cream. Add more salt and sugar to taste.

M. Miller, Wooster, OH

CHEESY CREAMED CORN

6 cups fresh or frozen corn	6 slices American cheese
1 (8 ounce) package cream cheese	1 clove garlic, minced
	1 teaspoon salt
¼ cup butter	Dash pepper

Thaw corn, if frozen. Combine all ingredients and put into slow cooker. Cook on low for 4 hours, stirring 1 or 2 times. Stir well before serving. You can also pour ingredients into greased casserole dish and bake at 350 degrees for 25 to 30 minutes or until bubbly around the edges. Optional: Combine 2 sleeves Ritz crackers and 2 tablespoons browned butter for topping to add just before serving.

Katie Zook, Apple Creek, OH

CORN PUDDING

3 eggs, beaten	2 tablespoons butter
3 cups milk	½ cup chopped celery
2 tablespoons sugar	½ cup chopped onion
1 teaspoon salt	2 cups corn

Combine ingredients in casserole dish; bake at 350 degrees for 1 hour.

Mary Grace Peachey, Catlett, VA

Corn Fritters

1 pint sweet corn (fresh,
   frozen, or canned and
   drained)
½ cup flour
¼ cup crushed cracker
   crumbs

½ teaspoon baking soda
½ teaspoon pepper
1 teaspoon salt
1 egg, beaten
¼ to ½ cup milk
Lard or oil

Combine all ingredients along with just enough milk to make it hold together but not be too runny. Drop by tablespoonfuls onto hot griddle greased with lard. Fry on both sides. Good served with applesauce or tomatoes.

Rachel Yutzy, Nickerson, KS

Apple Corn Bread

¾ cup cornmeal
¾ cup spelt or whole wheat
 flour
3 teaspoons baking powder
¼ teaspoon ground cloves
1 teaspoon cinnamon
¾ teaspoon salt

1 egg, beaten
1 teaspoon vanilla
¾ cup buttermilk
2 tablespoons oil or butter
1 tablespoon honey
2 cups diced apples

Sift dry ingredients together. Add egg, vanilla, and buttermilk. Blend well.
Add oil, honey, and apples. Mix thoroughly. Pour into greased 9-inch
square pan. Bake at 350 degrees for 25 minutes.

Phebe Peight, McVeytown, PA

Dandelion Gravy

3 to 4 slices bacon
½ cup chopped onion
2 tablespoons flour
1 cup milk
1 tablespoon vinegar
(optional)

2 hard-boiled eggs, chopped
Salt and pepper
2 to 3 cups chopped tender
spring dandelion leaves
(before it flowers)

Fry bacon and onion in a skillet until bacon is crisp and onions are browned; set aside, reserving bacon grease in skillet. Add flour to grease. Cook gently until lightly browned. Slowly add milk, stirring until smooth and thickened. Add vinegar, eggs, bacon, and onions. Season to taste with salt and pepper. Add dandelion leaves. As soon as leaves wilt, it is ready. Can be served on toast or with potatoes, mashed or fried.

Fried Pink Tomatoes

4 slices bacon
Pink tomatoes (not quite ripe)
Flour
Salt

Oregano (optional)
1 to 2 tablespoons flour
1 to 2 cups milk
Salt and pepper

Fry bacon in large skillet, crumble, and keep warm. Leave enough grease in pan to fry tomatoes. Save extra grease. Slice enough tomatoes to cover serving platter. Do not peel. Dip slices into flour and fry until golden brown on both sides. Salt and sprinkle with oregano to taste. Place on warm platter and keep warm. Put enough grease back in pan to moisten. Add 1 to 2 tablespoons flour. Slowly stir in milk (1 cup per tablespoon of flour). Cook until thickened. Salt and pepper to taste. Pour gravy over platter of tomatoes. Sprinkle bacon on top. Can be served with rice.

Anna Zook, Dalton, OH

Tomato Fritters

2 cups canned or fresh
   tomatoes, diced or mashed
2 eggs, beaten
2 tablespoons margarine,
   melted

½ teaspoon salt
2 tablespoons tomato juice
½ cup plus 2 tablespoons
   flour
Margarine or oil for frying

Combine tomatoes and egg; mix in margarine and salt. Stir in tomato juice then flour until there are no lumps. Melt margarine in frying pan. Pour batter into pan in pancake-sized fritters. Fry until tops and edges are covered with bubbles and edges are browned. Flip and cook until browned.

Mary H. Miller, Heuvelton, NY

Stewed Tomatoes

1 quart canned tomatoes
1 teaspoon salt
¼ cup sugar
1 tablespoon butter

2 tablespoons flour
½ cup milk
Soda crackers or bread

In medium saucepan, cook tomatoes with salt for 15 minutes. Add sugar and butter. In separate bowl, slowly combine flour and milk until there are no lumps. Add floury milk to tomatoes, stirring over medium heat until thickened. To serve, break up crackers or bread in serving dish and pour tomatoes over them. Stir and serve.

FRIED EGGPLANT

12 slices eggplant, ⅛-inch thick	¼ cup (scant) milk
3 eggs	Butter
	Cracker crumbs, crushed fine

Peel and slice eggplant starting at narrow end. Beat together eggs and milk. In skillet, heat butter over medium heat. Dip eggplant in egg mixture then in cracker crumbs. Fry until golden brown on both sides. Serve with tomato slices on bread with salad dressing.

Esther Keim, Ashland, OH

Eggplant Casserole

1 eggplant
1 egg
Milk (optional)
Oil

1 cup cracker crumbs
2 to 3 tomatoes
1 pound Velveeta or
American cheese

Peel eggplant and cut into slices ¼-inch thick. Beat egg. Add a little milk to egg if needed. Heat skillet with plenty of oil. Dip eggplant slices into egg, then into cracker crumbs. Sprinkle with salt and fry on both sides until soft. Make several alternating layers in casserole dish with eggplant, peeled slices of tomato, then cheese. Press down with hands to compact layers. Cover and bake at 350 degrees for 30 to 45 minutes.

Anna M. Byler, Belleville, PA

GREEN BEANS 3 WAYS

CRUMBED:

4 cups cooked green beans, drained

6 tablespoons fat

½ cup bread crumbs

Salt and pepper, to taste

Heat beans in fat. Add crumbs, salt, and pepper, stirring until beans are coated with crumbs and browned.

WITH FRIED ONIONS:

1 onion, sliced or chopped

Butter

Sage

4 cups cooked green beans, drained

Salt and pepper

In frying pan, fry onion in butter with a little sage. When tender, combine with beans and season to taste with salt and pepper.

CREAMED:

4 cups green beans

Milk

Butter

Salt and pepper

Cornstarch

Cook fresh beans until tender (or use canned beans). Pour about half the cooking water off; add milk almost to top of beans. Add butter, salt, and pepper to your taste. Cornstarch can be stirred in to thicken mixture.

Mary H. Miller, Heuvelton, NY

Green Bean Casserole

2 pounds hamburger
1 large onion, chopped
1 quart green beans
2 cups tomato soup or juice
1 cup sliced carrots, cooked
2 cups white sauce (recipe below)
2 cups mashed potatoes
Shredded cheese (optional)

Brown hamburger and onion; drain. Add green beans, tomato soup, carrots, and white sauce; pour into casserole dish and top with mashed potatoes. Optional: Mix some shredded cheese in with white sauce or top potatoes with cheese during last 15 minutes of baking. Bake at 350 degrees for 30 minutes until nicely browned and bubbly.

White Sauce:

4 tablespoons butter
4 tablespoons flour
½ teaspoon salt
2 cups milk

Melt butter in saucepan; mix in flour and salt. Slowly add milk and cook until thickened. Yields 2 cups.

Mary Grace Peachey, Catlett, VA

All-Day Beans

1 pound dry beans (navy and/or others)
½ pound bacon, fried and crumbled
1 large onion, chopped
1 cup brown sugar
1 teaspoon dry mustard
1 teaspoon cinnamon
Salt and pepper, to taste

Soak beans overnight in water. Boil for 30 minutes. Pour off water. Add fresh water to cover; mix in remaining ingredients. Put into baking dish and bake slowly between 250 and 325 degrees for several hours.

Alma Gingerich, Irvona, PA

Flavored Green Beans

Bacon
Onions
2 quarts green beans
½ teaspoon garlic powder

1 teaspoon dry mustard
½ cup brown sugar
¼ cup vinegar

Brown bacon and onion in bottom of pot. Mix in remaining ingredients and steam till tender, or if using canned beans, just heat thoroughly.

Polly Miller, Topeka, IN

Barbecued Green Beans

1 quart canned green beans
1 small onion, chopped
¾ cup brown sugar

6 slices bacon, lightly cooked
  and cut into pieces
1 cup ketchup

Mix all ingredients and bake in covered casserole dish at 350 degrees for 1 hour.

Mrs. John Mast, Kalona, IA

Sloppy Potatoes

3 medium potatoes, sliced
1 medium onion, sliced
1 tablespoon butter

½ teaspoon salt
½ cup water

In medium saucepan, bring all ingredients to a boil. Reduce to low and cook 15 minutes, stirring occasionally.

Potato Pancakes

3 cups shredded potatoes
2 eggs, beaten
1½ tablespoons flour

⅛ teaspoon baking powder
1 teaspoon salt
Oil or butter

Combine potatoes and eggs; stir in dry ingredients. Fry in hot oil as you would for pancakes.

Laura Hershberger, Howard, OH

CRUNCHY POTATO BALLS

2 cups stiff mashed potatoes
2 cups finely chopped ham
1 cup shredded cheddar or
  swiss cheese
⅓ cup mayonnaise
1 egg, beaten
1 teaspoon mustard
¼ teaspoon pepper
2 to 4 tablespoons flour
1¾ cups cornflakes, crushed

In bowl, combine potatoes, ham, cheese, mayonnaise, egg, mustard, and pepper; mix well. Add enough flour to make batter stiff. Chill. Make balls from batter with cookie scoop. Roll in cornflakes. Place on greased baking sheet. Bake at 350 degrees for 25 to 30 minutes. Serve hot.

Vera Mast, Kalona, IA

MASHED POTATO CASSEROLE

¾ cup chopped onion
½ cup butter
8 cups cubed ham
  (approximately 4 pounds)
3 cups cream of mushroom
  soup
3 cups cubed Velveeta cheese
  (1½ pounds)
2 tablespoons Worcestershire
  sauce
¾ teaspoon pepper
6 quarts mashed potatoes
  (without any milk or salt)
3 cups sour cream
1 to 2 pounds bacon, cooked
  and crumbled

Sauté onion in butter; add ham, mushroom soup, cheese, Worcestershire sauce, and pepper. Place in large roaster. Mix mashed potatoes and sour cream; spread on meat mixture. Top with bacon. Bake at 350 degrees for 1 hour.

Sharon Mishler, Lagrange, IN

POTLUCK POTATOES

2 pounds potatoes
2 tablespoons butter
1 medium onion, chopped
1 can cream of mushroom
  soup
1 pint sour cream
2 cups Velveeta cheese

1 teaspoon salt
1 teaspoon pepper
2 cups cornflakes or potato
  chips, crushed
½ cup butter, melted
2 tablespoons sour cream
Onion powder

Cook potatoes until almost tender; shred. In saucepan, melt butter and cook onions lightly; add mushroom soup, sour cream, and cheese. Cook over low heat until combined. Add salt and pepper. Combine with potatoes. Pour into casserole dish. Bake at 350 degrees until heated through. Mix cornflakes, butter, sour cream, and onion powder to taste. Spread over top. Bake until browned.

Mrs. Joseph Miller, Navarre, OH

ONION PATTIES

¾ cup flour
1 tablespoon sugar
1 tablespoon cornmeal
2 teaspoons baking powder

⅓ teaspoon salt
¾ cup milk
2½ cups finely chopped onion
Oil

Mix together flour, sugar, cornmeal, baking powder, salt, and milk. Batter should be fairly thick. Add onion and then drop by spoonfuls into hot oil. Fry till golden brown on both sides; press to flatten when turned.

Ida Hochstetler, Shipshewana, IN

Seasoned Potato Wedges

½ cup butter, melted
¼ cup flour
¾ cup grated Parmesan
   cheese
1 tablespoon paprika

¾ teaspoon salt
⅛ teaspoon pepper
6 medium (2 pounds)
   potatoes, peeled and
   quartered lengthwise

Mix all ingredients but potatoes together in large plastic bag. Insert potatoes; shake to coat. Place potatoes on baking sheet; bake uncovered at 350 degrees for 50 to 60 minutes, turning after 30 minutes.

Susan Schwartz, Berne, IN

CARAMELIZED SWEET POTATOES

Sweet potatoes
3 tablespoons butter
1½ cups water or milk

1 tablespoon cornstarch
½ cup brown sugar
Pinch salt

Cook sweet potatoes to your preference by baking, boiling, or frying. Slice and place in serving dish. In pan, brown butter; add water and bring to a boil. Mix together cornstarch, brown sugar, and salt with a bit of water to make a paste. Add to saucepan mixture and return to a boil. Pour over sweet potatoes.

Elizabeth Miller, Brown City, MI

Sweet Potatoes

Peel and slice sweet potatoes (½-inch thick). Dip slices in flour, then fry in butter on stovetop until very lightly browned. To finish cooking, place slices on cookie sheet. Salt lightly. Bake uncovered in oven at 350 degrees for 15 to 20 minutes or until soft. Serve with extra butter.

Ruby Borntrager, Goshen, IN

Zucchini Patties

1 cup shredded zucchini	2 tablespoons diced onion
1 egg	(optional)
1 teaspoon salt	Oil or butter
1 cup cracker crumbs	Slices of cheese

Mix together zucchini, egg, salt, cracker crumbs, and onion; form into patties. Pan fry in oil or butter until brown on both sides. Melt a slice of cheese on top of each patty. Serve topped with lettuce, tomato, and onion.

Emma Sue Schwartz, South Whitley, IN

Zucchini Casserole

3 cups shredded zucchini	¾ teaspoon salt
½ cup oil	½ teaspoon garlic powder
2 tablespoons flour	½ cup shredded cheese
¾ cup quick oats	

Combine all ingredients. Pour into baking dish. Bake at 350 degrees for 30 minutes to 1 hour.

Emma Sue Schwartz, South Whitley, IN

Baked Squash

1 medium butternut or
    buttercup squash
2 sleeves saltine crackers,
    crushed fine
2 cups cornflakes, crushed

2 teaspoons salt
1 teaspoon seasoned salt
½ teaspoon paprika
½ cup butter, melted

Cut squash in half and remove seeds and skin. Cut into ½-inch slices. Mix crackers, cornflakes, salt, seasoned salt, and paprika. Dip each piece of squash into butter then roll in crumb mixture. Place on cookie sheet in a single layer. Bake at 350 degrees 1 to 1½ hours until tender.

M. Weaver, Michigan

Vegetable Nut Pancakes

1 cup milk
3 tablespoons oil
1 egg, beaten
1 cup rice flour
½ teaspoon salt

1 tablespoon baking powder
½ cup chopped celery
½ cup chopped carrots
1 cup chopped nuts

Combine milk, oil, and egg; add flour, salt, and baking powder and mix well. Stir in vegetables and nuts. Fry slowly in hot oiled skillet.

Anna Zook, Dalton, OH

Summer Zucchini Casserole

⅓ cup olive oil
2 tablespoons wine vinegar
2 tablespoons parsley
3 teaspoons salt
¾ teaspoon pepper
1 teaspoon hot sauce
1 medium zucchini, chopped
2 white potatoes, chopped
2 small green peppers, chopped
2 carrots, chopped
1 celery stalk, chopped
3 to 4 medium tomatoes, sliced thin
½ cup uncooked rice (not instant)
1¾ cups shredded cheddar cheese

Blend oil, vinegar, parsley, salt, pepper, and hot sauce; set aside. Mix zucchini, potatoes, peppers, carrots, and celery in large bowl. Spray large casserole dish with oil. Cover bottom with layer of sliced tomatoes. Cover with half the vegetables. Place another layer of tomatoes. Sprinkle with rice. Add remaining vegetables and top with final layer of tomatoes. Stir oil mixture and pour over all. Cover with foil and bake 1¼ hours at 350 degrees. Remove foil and sprinkle with cheese. Bake another 15 minutes.

PEAS · BROCOLLI · CARROTS · CAULIFLOWER · SPINACH · CABBAGE · BEETS · POTA
uliflower · spinach · cabbage · beets · potatoes · onions · apples · turnips · lettuce
SH · RUTABAGA · PEAS · BROCOLLI · CARROTS · CAULIFLOWER · SPINACH · CABBA
spinach · cabbage · beets · potatoes · onions · apples · turnips · lettuce · garlic · toma
N · YAMS · SQUASH · RUTABAGA · PEAS · BROCOLLI · CARROTS · CAULIFLOWER · SP
bbage · beets · potatoes · onions · apples · turnips · lettuce · garlic · tomatoes · zucchini
· BEANS · CORN · YAMS · SQUASH · RUTABAGA · PEAS · BROCOLLI · CARROTS
toes · onions · apples · turnips · lettuce · garlic · tomatoes · zucchini · cucumbers · bea
UCCHINI · CUCUMBERS · BEANS · CORN · YAMS · SQUASH · RUTABAGA · PEAS · B
ples · turnips · lettuce · garlic · tomatoes · zucchini · cucumbers · beans · corn · yams
RLIC · TOMATOES · ZUCCHINI · CUCUMBERS · BEANS · CORN · YAMS · SQUASH · P
lettuce · garlic · tomatoes · zucchini · cucumbers · beans · corn · yams · squash · rutabag
NIPS · LETTUCE · GARLIC · TOMATOES · ZUCCHINI · CUCUMBERS · BEANS · CORN
matoes · zucchini · cucumbers · beans · corn · yams · squash · rutabaga · peas · brocolli
NIONS · APPLES · TURNIPS · LETTUCE · GARLIC · TOMATOES · ZUCCHINI · CUCUMB
cucumbers · beans · corn · yams · squash · rutabaga · peas · brocolli · carrots · caul
ETS · POTATOES · ONIONS · APPLES · TURNIPS · LETTUCE · GARLIC · TOMATOES · ZUC
· beans · corn · yams · squash · rutabaga · peas · brocolli · carrots · cauliflower · spi
ABBAGE · BEETS · POTATOES · ONIONS · APPLES · TURNIPS · LETTUCE · GARLIC · TO
· yams · squash · rutabaga · peas · brocolli · carrots · cauliflower · spinach · cabbage
R · SPINACH · CABBAGE · BEETS · POTATOES · ONIONS · APPLES · TURNIPS · LETT
sh · rutabaga · peas · brocolli · carrots · cauliflower · spinach · cabbage · beets · potat
RROTS · CAULIFLOWER · SPINACH · CABBAGE · BEETS · POTATOES · ONIONS · APP
peas · brocolli · carrots · cauliflower · spinach · cabbage · beets · potatoes · onions · o
EAS · BROCOLLI · CARROTS · CAULIFLOWER · SPINACH · CABBAGE · BEETS · POTATO
lli · carrots · cauliflower · spinach · cabbage · beets · potatoes · onions · apples · turni
SH · RUTABAGA · PEAS · BROCOLLI · CARROTS · CAULIFLOWER · SPINACH · CABBAG
auliflower · spinach · cabbage · beets · potatoes · onions · apples · turnips · lettuce
N · YAMS · SQUASH · RUTABAGA · PEAS · BROCOLLI · CARROTS · CAULIFLOWER · SP
· spinach · cabbage · beets · potatoes · onions · apples · turnips · lettuce · garlic · toma
· BEANS · CORN · YAMS · SQUASH · RUTABAGA · PEAS · BROCOLLI · CARROTS
bbage · beets · potatoes · onions · apples · turnips · lettuce · garlic · tomatoes · zucchini
UCCHINI · CUCUMBERS · BEANS · CORN · YAMS · SQUASH · RUTABAGA · PEAS · B
atoes · onions · apples · turnips · lettuce · garlic · tomatoes · zucchini · cucumbers · bea
RLIC · TOMATOES · ZUCCHINI · CUCUMBERS · BEANS · CORN · YAMS · SQUASH · P
ples · turnips · lettuce · garlic · tomatoes · zucchini · cucumbers · beans · corn · yams
NIPS · LETTUCE · GARLIC · TOMATOES · ZUCCHINI · CUCUMBERS · BEANS · CORN
lettuce · garlic · tomatoes · zucchini · cucumbers · beans · corn · yams · squash · rutabag
NIONS · APPLES · TURNIPS · LETTUCE · GARLIC · TOMATOES · ZUCCHINI · CUCUME
matoes · zucchini · cucumbers · beans · corn · yams · squash · rutabaga · peas · brocolli
ETS · POTATOES · ONIONS · APPLES · TURNIPS · LETTUCE · GARLIC · TOMATOES · ZUC
cucumbers · beans · corn · yams · squash · rutabaga · peas · brocolli · carrots · caul
ABBAGE · BEETS · POTATOES · ONIONS · APPLES · TURNIPS · LETTUCE · GARLIC · TO
· beans · corn · yams · squash · rutabaga · peas · brocolli · carrots · cauliflower · spi
R · SPINACH · CABBAGE · BEETS · POTATOES · ONIONS · APPLES · TURNIPS · LETT
· yams · squash · rutabaga · peas · brocolli · carrots · cauliflower · spinach · cabbag
RROTS · CAULIFLOWER · SPINACH · CABBAGE · BEETS · POTATOES · ONIONS · APP
sh · rutabaga · peas · brocolli · carrots · cauliflower · spinach · cabbage · beets · potat
EAS · BROCOLLI · CARROTS · CAULIFLOWER · SPINACH · CABBAGE · BEETS · POTAT
peas · brocolli · carrots · cauliflower · spinach · cabbage · beets · potatoes · onions
SH · RUTABAGA · PEAS · BROCOLLI · CARROTS · CAULIFLOWER · SPINACH · CABBAG
lli · carrots · cauliflower · spinach · cabbage · beets · potatoes · onions · apples · turni
· YAMS · SQUASH · RUTABAGA · PEAS · BROCOLLI · CARROTS · CAULIFLOWER

Recipes for Desserts

My son, eat thou honey, because it is good;
and the honeycomb, which is sweet to thy taste.

Proverbs 24:13

APPLE BARS

1 cup flour
1 cup oats
1 cup brown sugar, divided
½ teaspoon baking soda
½ teaspoon salt
½ cup butter
2½ cups finely chopped apples
2 tablespoons butter, cut

Mix flour, oats, ½ cup brown sugar, baking soda, salt, and ½ cup butter until crumbly. Press half of mixture into 8 x 8-inch pan. Combine apples and ½ cup brown sugar; spread over crust. Dot with butter. Top with remaining crumb mixture. Bake at 350 degrees for 40 minutes or until golden brown. Serve warm with milk or ice cream.

Esther P. Mast, Gambier, OH

APPLE CRISP

2 quarts apple pie filling
1 rounded cup butter, melted
1 teaspoon salt
1 cup honey
¾ cup wheat bran
5 cups quick oats
3 cups wheat flour

Put apple pie filling on bottom of 10 x 14-inch pan. Mix remaining ingredients together and cover filling. Bake at 350 degrees for 35 minutes until bubbly around the edges.

Fran Nissley, Campbellsville, KY

APPLE WALNUT COBBLER

4 cups sliced tart apples
1¼ cups sugar, divided
½ teaspoon cinnamon
¾ cup coarsely chopped
    walnuts, divided
1 cup flour

1 teaspoon baking powder
¼ teaspoon salt
1 egg, well beaten
½ cup evaporated milk
⅓ cup butter, melted

Place apples in bottom of greased 8-inch square baking dish. Mix ½ cup sugar, cinnamon, and ½ cup nuts; sprinkle over apples. Sift together remaining ¾ cup sugar, flour, baking powder, and salt. In mixing bowl, combine egg, milk, and butter; add flour mixture and blend until smooth. Pour over apples. Sprinkle with remaining ¼ cup nuts. Bake at 350 degrees for 50 minutes. Serve with whipped cream sprinkled with cinnamon.

Lois Rhodes, Harrisonburg, VA

Apple Blossom Cake

1¼ cups oil
2 cups sugar
2 eggs
1 teaspoon vanilla
3 cups flour
½ teaspoon salt

1½ teaspoons baking soda
1 teaspoon cinnamon
1 teaspoon nutmeg
1 cup chopped nuts
3 cups peeled and chopped apples

Topping:

½ cup sugar
1 teaspoon cinnamon

½ cup chopped nuts

Beat together oil, sugar, eggs, and vanilla. Add flour, salt, baking soda, cinnamon, and nutmeg. Fold in nuts and apples. Pour into greased 9 x 13-inch pan. Combine topping ingredients and sprinkle over batter. Bake at 350 degrees for 35 to 40 minutes.

Lucy Wengerd, Monroe, IN

Apple Dapple Cake

2 eggs
2 cups sugar
1 cup oil
3 cups flour
1 teaspoon baking soda

½ teaspoon salt
3 cups shredded apples
2 teaspoons vanilla
Nuts (optional)

Blend eggs, sugar, and oil. Sift together flour, baking soda, and salt; add to egg mixture. Add apples, vanilla, and nuts. Mix well. Bake in large greased cake pan at 350 degrees for 45 minutes.

Icing:

1 cup brown sugar
¼ cup milk

¼ cup butter

Cook for 2½ minutes. Stir a little after removing from heat, but do not beat. Dapple over cake while cake and icing are still hot. Sprinkle additional nuts on top if desired. Also tastes good without icing.

Elizabeth Shetler, Brinkhaven, OH

Pear Cake

2 cups coarsely chopped
   pears, no juice
1 teaspoon baking soda
¼ cup shortening
1¼ cups sugar

1 egg
1 cup flour
¼ teaspoon salt
1 teaspoon cinnamon

Combine pears and baking soda; set aside. Cream together shortening and sugar; add egg and mix well. Sift together flour, salt, and cinnamon; add to creamed mixture. Fold in pears. Bake at 350 degrees for 50 minutes. Best served warm with milk.

Esther Schlabach, Vanleer, TN

BLACKBERRY PUDDING COBBLER

⅓ cup butter
2 cups sugar, divided
2 cups flour
1 teaspoon salt

2 teaspoons baking powder
1 cup milk
2 cups fresh or frozen
  blackberries
2 cups boiling water

Cream butter and 1 cup sugar together. Add flour, salt, baking powder, and milk. Mix well and spread into greased 9 x 13-inch pan. Pour blackberries on top of batter. Combine remaining 1 cup sugar and 2 cups boiling water and pour over berries. Bake for 50 minutes. Note: Other fruit or berries may be substituted for the blackberries.

Mrs. Paul Schrock, Marion, MI

BLUEBERRY CREAM PIE

1 cup sour cream
1 cup sugar
2 tablespoons flour
1 teaspoon vanilla
¼ teaspoon salt

1 egg
1 cup blueberries
1 unbaked piecrust
3 tablespoons flour
1½ tablespoons butter

Beat together sour cream, sugar, flour, vanilla, salt, and egg. Fold in blueberries. Pour into unbaked piecrust. Bake at 350 degrees for 50 minutes. Top with mixture of flour and butter. Brown in oven.

Susan Mast, Danville, OH

Swedish Apple Pudding

1½ cups sugar	6 apples, chopped
2 eggs	2 teaspoons baking soda
2 cups flour	1 teaspoon nutmeg
2 teaspoons cinnamon	¼ teaspoon salt
⅔ cup shortening	

Put ingredients in bowl in order given. Mix well. Pour into greased 9 x 13-inch pan. Bake at 350 degrees for 1 hour.

Sauce:

1½ cups brown sugar	2 tablespoons butter
2 tablespoons flour	1 teaspoon vanilla or maple
1 cup water	flavoring

Cook all together until thick. Cool and pour over cake.

Thelma Zook, Oakland, MD

Fresh Blueberry Crisp Dessert

5 cups blueberries
1¼ cups brown sugar, divided
2 tablespoons Minute Tapioca
½ cup water

1 teaspoon lemon juice
  (optional)
½ cup melted butter
1 cup flour
1 cup quick oats

Combine berries, ¾ cup brown sugar, tapioca, water, and lemon juice and pour into greased 9 x 13-inch baking dish. In bowl, mix butter, ½ cup brown sugar, flour, and oats. Sprinkle over blueberry mixture. Bake at 350 degrees for 40 minutes. Serve warm with ice cream or milk.

Esther Peachey, Flemingsburg, KY

BLUEBERRY DELIGHT

1½ cups flour
1 cup chopped nuts

½ cup butter

Mix crust and pat into 9 x 13-inch pan. Bake at 350 degrees for 13 minutes. Let cool.

1 (8 ounce) package cream
cheese

2 cups whipped topping

Beat together and spread on top of cooled crust.

6 cups water
¾ cup sugar
½ cup Perma-flo

6 ounces grape gelatin
powder
Blueberries

Bring water to a boil. Add sugar and Perma-flo, cook until thickened. Stir in gelatin. Cool and add fruit. Spread over cheese layer. Chill several hours before serving.

You can use any combination of fruit and gelatin. With peaches, try 3 ounces orange and 3 ounces mango gelatin.

Mary Mast, Hamptonville, NC

FRUIT TAPIOCA

10 cups water
1 cup granulated tapioca
2 cups sugar

½ teaspoon salt
2 quarts fresh fruit
(raspberries, blackberries,
peaches, or other)

Bring water to a boil. Add tapioca; cook until clear. Remove from heat and add sugar, salt, and fruit.

Alvin and Katie Hertzler, Salisbury, PA

Carrot Cake

2 cups flour
1½ cups sugar
½ teaspoon salt
1 teaspoon cinnamon
1 teaspoon nutmeg
1 teaspoon ground cloves

½ teaspoon baking soda
1 teaspoon baking powder
¾ cup oil
4 eggs
3 cups grated carrots (can also use zucchini or sweet potatoes)

Mix flour, sugar, salt, cinnamon, nutmeg, cloves, baking soda, and baking powder. Add oil and eggs; mix well. Add carrots; mix well. Pour into greased 9 x 13-inch pan (or use jelly roll sheet to serve as bars). Bake at 350 degrees for around 45 minutes (30 minutes for bars). Cool and frost with your favorite icing.

Mrs. Raymond Kauffman, Laplata, MO

Cherry Melt Away Bars

2 cups flour
2 eggs, separated
1½ cups sugar, divided
1 cup margarine or butter

2 cans or 1 quart cherry pie filling
Dash cream of tartar
1 teaspoon vanilla
½ cup chopped nuts

Cream together flour, egg yolks, 1 cup sugar, and margarine. Press into 9 x 13-inch pan. Spread pie filling on crust. Beat egg whites with cream of tartar until very stiff. Gradually beat in ½ cup sugar then vanilla. Spread over pie filling. Sprinkle with nuts. Bake at 350 degrees for 30 to 35 minutes.

Mattie Yoder, Fairchild, WI

FRUIT PIZZA

CRUST:

½ cup butter
¾ cup sugar
1 egg

1½ cups flour
1 teaspoon baking powder
¼ teaspoon salt

Cream butter, sugar, and egg together and then add remaining ingredients. Bake on 14-inch pan at 350 degrees for 12 minutes. Remove from oven; let cool.

CREAM LAYER:

1 (8 ounce) package cream cheese
½ cup sugar

1 (8 ounce) package whipped topping
Vanilla, to taste

Mix together and spread on crust.

FRUIT LAYER:

Layer on any fruits of your choice, cut or whole.

GLAZE:

1¾ cups white sugar
¼ teaspoon salt
1 envelope Kool-Aid (any flavor)

4 cups water
¾ cup Clear Jel
½ cup water

Mix first 3 ingredients in saucepan and add to water, stir well, and bring to a boil. Mix Clear Jel with ½ cup water; add to boiling sauce, stirring constantly until thickened. Cool. Spread over top of fruit pizza.

Leona Mullet, Burton, OH

Green Tomato Bars

4 cups green tomatoes, finely chopped
2 cups brown sugar, divided
¾ cup butter, softened
1½ cups flour
1 teaspoon baking soda
1 teaspoon salt
2 cups oats
½ cup nuts, chopped
1 cup blueberries (fresh or frozen), optional

In saucepan, cook tomatoes and 1 cup brown sugar over low heat until tomatoes are softened and juicy. In mixing bowl, cream butter and remaining sugar together; add flour, baking soda, salt, oats, and nuts. Grease 9 x 13-inch pan. Measure out 2½ cups dough and press into bottom of pan. Spread tomato mixture, including juice, on top. Sprinkle optional berries over tomatoes. Crumble remaining dough and sprinkle over all. Bake at 375 degrees for 30 to 35 minutes.

The blueberries help to hide the green from the kids and make the bars more appealing to the eye. Still just as yummy without the berries, though.

Fresh Peach Pie

6 peaches, sliced
1 unbaked piecrust
¼ cup flour
¾ cup sugar
1 cup cream
⅓ cup flour
⅓ cup sugar
3 tablespoons butter

Arrange peaches in piecrust. Mix ¼ cup flour, ¾ cup sugar, and cream. Pour over peaches. Combine ⅓ cup flour, ⅓ cup sugar, and butter; crumble on top of pie. Bake at 425 degrees for 10 minutes. Lower heat to 350 degrees and bake for 30 minutes, or until filling is set.

Mrs. Joseph Schwartz, Salem, IN

Famous Lemon Pie

3 tablespoons cornstarch	¼ cup cold water
1¼ cups sugar	1½ cups boiling water
¼ cup lemon juice	1 baked piecrust
3 eggs, separated	¼ cup sugar

Mix cornstarch, 1¼ cups sugar, lemon juice, and egg yolks in cold water; pour into boiling water, stirring until thickened. Pour into baked piecrust. Beat egg whites until stiff; add ¼ cup sugar. Spread on top of pie. Bake at 325 degrees for 15 to 18 minutes or until browned.

Susanna Mast, Kalona, IA

Peach Bavarian Mold

1 pint canned sliced peaches
  in syrup
2 (3 ounce) packages peach or
  apricot gelatin
½ cup sugar
2 cups boiling water

1 teaspoon almond extract
1 (8 ounce) carton whipped
  topping, or 8 ounces
  whipping cream, whipped
Peach slices (optional)

Drain peaches, reserving ⅔ cup juice. Chop peaches into small pieces; set aside. In bowl, dissolve gelatin and sugar in boiling water. Stir in reserved juice. Chill until slightly thickened. Combine extract with whipped topping; gently fold into gelatin. Fold in peach slices. Pour into oiled 6-cup mold. Chill overnight. Unmold; garnish with additional peaches, if desired. Yield: 8 to 10 servings.

Variation: Use different flavors of gelatin and fruits. Put cottage cheese between 2 layers of the gelatin mixture.

Martha Petersheim, Verdigre, NE

Sour Cream Pear Pie

2 cups peeled and diced ripe
  pears
1 cup sugar, divided
1 egg, beaten
1 tablespoon flour
1 cup sour cream
1 teaspoon vanilla
Dash salt
1 (9-inch) unbaked piecrust
⅓ cup flour
¼ cup butter, softened

Combine pears, ½ cup sugar, egg, flour, sour cream, vanilla, and salt. Blend gently. Spoon into unbaked piecrust. Bake at 350 degrees for 25 minutes. Combine ½ cup sugar, flour, and butter. Sprinkle on pie. Return to oven for 30 minutes more.

Mary Ellen Wengerd, Campbellsville, KY

Pumpkin Bread

4 eggs
3 cups sugar
1 teaspoon cinnamon
⅔ cup water
1 cup olive oil
1 cup chopped nuts
½ teaspoon salt
1 teaspoon nutmeg
2 cups pumpkin puree
2 teaspoons baking soda
3½ cups flour

In large bowl, beat eggs; add remaining ingredients and mix well. Pour into 3 well-greased loaf pans. Bake at 300 degrees for 1 hour or until done in center. This bread freezes well.

Katie Yoder, Fultonville, NY

Harvest Loaf

1¾ cups flour
1 teaspoon baking soda
1 teaspoon cinnamon
½ teaspoon nutmeg
¼ teaspoon ginger
¼ teaspoon ground cloves

½ cup butter
1 cup sugar
2 eggs
¾ cup pumpkin puree
½ cup chocolate chips
¼ cup raisins or nuts

Mix all ingredients together. Bake in greased loaf pan at 350 degrees for 60 minutes.

Mary Jane Kuepfer, Chesley, Ontario, Canada

Country Pumpkin Muffins

2 cups sugar
½ cup oil
2 eggs
2 cups pumpkin puree
3 cups flour
½ teaspoon baking powder
1 teaspoon baking soda

½ teaspoon ground cloves
¾ teaspoon cinnamon
½ teaspoon nutmeg
1 teaspoon salt
1½ cups raisins
1 cup chopped walnuts

Mix sugar, oil, eggs, and pumpkin. Combine flour, baking powder, baking soda, and spices. Add dry mix to pumpkin mixture. Fold in raisins and nuts. Bake in well-greased or lined muffin tins at 375 degrees for 15 minutes. Yields 2 dozen.

Amanda Kuepfer, Chesley, Ontario, Canada

Pumpkin Cookies

1 cup sugar	2 cups flour
½ cup butter	1 teaspoon baking soda
1 egg	½ teaspoon baking powder
1 teaspoon vanilla	1 teaspoon cinnamon
1 cup pumpkin puree	¼ teaspoon salt

Cream together sugar and butter. Add egg, vanilla, and pumpkin. Mix well. Combine flour, baking soda, baking powder, cinnamon, and salt. Add to pumpkin mixture. Drop dough by teaspoon amounts on cookie sheet lined with parchment paper. Bake at 350 degrees for 12 to 15 minutes. Cool and frost.

Frosting:

3 tablespoons butter	2 cups powdered sugar
4 tablespoons milk	1 teaspoon vanilla
½ cup brown sugar	

Boil butter, milk, and brown sugar for 2 minutes. Let cool and add powdered sugar and vanilla. Spread on cookies. Will be thin but will thicken as it cools on the cookies.

Rhonda Ropp, Crofton, KY

Pumpkin Fruitcake

1 cup sugar	1 teaspoon ground cloves
1 cup brown sugar	1 teaspoon nutmeg
¼ cup shortening	¼ teaspoon salt
2 eggs	15 ounces cooked pumpkin
2½ cups flour	1 cup raisins
2 teaspoons baking soda	1 cup chopped nuts
2 teaspoons cinnamon	1 cup chopped maraschino cherries

In large bowl, mix sugars, shortening, and eggs. Combine flour, baking soda, cinnamon, cloves, nutmeg, and salt. Alternate between adding dry ingredients and pumpkin to sugar mixture. Beat on low until well mixed. Fold in raisins, nuts, and cherries. Pour into greased and floured Bundt pan or two bread pans. Bake at 350 degrees for 1 hour or until a toothpick inserted in center comes out clean. Cool 10 minutes; remove from pan.

GLAZE:

Powdered sugar	1 cup lemon juice

Add enough powdered sugar to lemon juice to make thick syrup that can be poured over the warm cake. Cut several slits in cake so syrup can soak in. Let cool before serving.

Esther Schlabach, Vanleer, TN

Pumpkin Pie

2 cups pumpkin puree	4 eggs, separated
1 cup sugar	1 teaspoon vanilla
1¼ cups brown sugar	Molasses, to taste
1 heaping cup flour	½ teaspoon salt
5 cups milk, scalded	2 unbaked piecrusts

Combine all but egg whites. Beat egg whites to a peak and fold into pumpkin mixture. Pour into piecrusts. Bake at 450 degrees for 10 minutes. Reduce heat to 350 degrees for 40 to 50 minutes.

Mrs. Kenneth A. Schrock, Monroe, WI

Cheater's Pumpkin Pie

Crust:

½ cup oats	1 cup flour
½ cup butter	½ cup brown sugar

Mix until crumbly; press into 9 x 13-inch pan and bake at 350 degrees for 15 minutes.

Filling:

½ cup brown sugar	3 cups milk
3 tablespoons flour	1 cup pumpkin puree
1 teaspoon salt	½ cup sugar
½ teaspoon cinnamon	3 eggs, separated

Mix all ingredients except egg whites. Beat egg whites until fluffy; add to pumpkin mixture. Pour into crust and bake at 350 degrees for 20 to 30 minutes, until set.

Esther E. Byler, Big Prairie, OH

GRANDMA'S RHUBARB CAKE

1½ cups brown sugar
½ cup butter
1 cup milk
1 egg, beaten
1 teaspoon vanilla
2 cups flour

1 teaspoon baking soda
¼ teaspoon salt
2½ cups chopped rhubarb
½ cup sugar
1 teaspoon cinnamon

Mix brown sugar and butter together; add milk, egg, and vanilla. Blend in flour, baking soda, and salt. Fold in rhubarb. Spread into greased and floured 9 x 13-inch pan or Bundt pan. Combine sugar and cinnamon and sprinkle on top. Bake at 350 degrees for 30 to 35 minutes. Makes a very moist cake.

Mrs. Samuel Schwartz, Geneva, IN

Rhubarb Nut Bread

1½ cups brown sugar, firmly
    packed
⅓ cup oil
1 egg
1 cup sour milk
1 teaspoon vanilla
1 teaspoon baking soda

½ teaspoon salt
2½ cups flour
1½ cups finely chopped fresh
    rhubarb stalks
½ cup chopped pecans
½ cup white sugar
1 teaspoon cinnamon

Mix all ingredients together except for white sugar and cinnamon. Pour into 2 greased and floured loaf pans. Combine white sugar and cinnamon. Sprinkle on top of batter. Bake at 325 degrees for 40 minutes.

Edna Irene Miller, Arthur, IL

Raspberry Cobbler

1 quart canned raspberries
Cornstarch
3 eggs, beaten
1 cup sugar
5 tablespoons water

1 cup sifted flour
1 teaspoon baking powder
1 teaspoon vanilla
Pinch salt

Separate juice from canned raspberries; place juice in saucepan. Measure out 1 tablespoon cornstarch for each cup of juice. Blend cornstarch with 1 tablespoon cold water; add to hot juice and cook until slightly thickened. Combine juice and raspberries in bottom of 9 x 13-inch baking dish. Mix eggs, sugar, water, flour, baking powder, vanilla, and salt into batter. Spread or dollop batter onto raspberries. Bake at 350 degrees for 40 to 45 minutes.

Ruth Hochstettler, Dundee, OH

Rhubarb Pie

2½ cups finely chopped
   rhubarb stalk
1½ cups sugar
½ cup flour
½ cup sugar

2 tablespoons strawberry
   gelatin
½ teaspoon salt
3 cups full-fat milk or half-
   and-half
2 large unbaked piecrusts

Mix rhubarb and sugar; let set awhile. Mix flour, sugar, gelatin, salt, and milk. Add rhubarb. Fill 2 large unbaked piecrusts. Bake at 425 degrees for 10 minutes. Reduce heat to 350 degrees and bake for 30 minutes.

Malinda Stutzman, Navarre, OH

Rhubarb Pudding

2 cups chopped rhubarb
1 cup sugar
½ cup water
2 tablespoons butter
2 tablespoons cornstarch

⅛ teaspoon salt
¼ cup sugar
2 eggs, beaten
¼ cup milk

In saucepan, cook rhubarb with 1 cup sugar, water, and butter until tender. Blend cornstarch, salt, and ¼ cup sugar; add eggs and milk. Combine with rhubarb and cook until thick.

Mrs. Peter Landis, Brodhead, WI

Rhubarb Dumplings

2½ teaspoons lard	Butter, softened
2 cups whole wheat flour	Sugar (I use raw)
2 teaspoons baking powder	2 cups finely chopped
1 teaspoon salt	rhubarb
⅞ cup milk	Cinnamon

Cut lard into flour, baking powder, and salt; add milk and mix well. Roll dough out to ¼-inch thickness; spread with butter like you would on bread. Sprinkle with sugar, then rhubarb, then cinnamon. Roll dough into a log. Cut into slices about 1¼ inch thick. Line slices in baking pan and pour prepared sauce over them. Bake at 350 degrees for 35 to 40 minutes.

Sauce:

1 cup sugar (I use raw)	1 cup hot water
3 tablespoons flour	½ teaspoon butter
¼ teaspoon salt	⅛ teaspoon cinnamon

Combine all ingredients and bring to a boil for 3 minutes.

Alvin and Katie Hertzler, Salisbury, PA

Hand-Cranked French Strawberry Ice Cream

6 egg yolks	4 cups heavy cream
2 cups milk	2 cups crushed strawberries
1 cup sugar	1 tablespoon lemon juice
Pinch salt	

Mix egg yolks, milk, sugar, and salt in double boiler and heat until mixture forms thick custard. Cook until mixture coats back of a wooden spoon evenly. Allow to cool. Add heavy cream. Pour into ice cream freezer and crank until half frozen. Add crushed strawberries and lemon juice; continue cranking until frozen. Allow to ripen (rest) a few hours before serving. Yields 2½ quarts.

Mollie Stoltzfus, Charlotte Hall, MD

STRAWBERRY FREEZE

½ cup softened margarine or
  butter
½ cup chopped pecans
¼ cup brown sugar
1 cup flour

6 egg whites
1 cup sugar
1 quart strawberries, sliced
1 tablespoon lemon juice
2 cups whipped topping

Mix butter, pecans, brown sugar, and flour. Spread onto baking sheet
and bake at 300 degrees for 20 minutes. Stir often to keep crumbly; cool,
stirring often. Put half the crumbs into serving dish. Beat egg whites until
stiff; add sugar, continuing to beat. Fold in strawberries, lemon juice,
and whipped topping. Spread over crumbs in dish. Sprinkle top with
remaining crumbs. Freeze at least 5 hours before serving.

Mrs. Orie Detweiler, Inola, OK

STRAWBERRY LONG CAKE

2 cups flour
6 tablespoons sugar
4 teaspoons baking powder
¾ teaspoon salt
⅓ cup shortening
¾ cup milk

1 large egg, beaten
¼ cup butter, softened
¾ cup sugar
¼ cup flour
Strawberries
Milk

Combine 2 cups flour, 6 tablespoons sugar, baking powder, and salt; cut
in shortening. Mix in milk; add egg. Put into greased 9 x 13-inch pan.
Combine butter, ¾ cup sugar, and flour; sprinkle over batter. Bake at 350
degrees for 30 to 35 minutes until top is golden. Top each serving with
diced strawberries and serve with milk.

JoAnn Schrock, Monroe, WI

STRAWBERRY PIE WITH CREAMY SATIN FILLING

½ cup sugar
3 tablespoons cornstarch
3 tablespoons flour
½ teaspoon salt
2 cups milk
1 egg, beaten
½ cup whipping cream, whipped

1 teaspoon vanilla
1 baked piecrust
½ cup sliced strawberries
½ cup water
¼ cup sugar
2 teaspoons cornstarch
Red food coloring

In saucepan, mix ½ cup sugar, 3 tablespoons cornstarch, flour, and salt; gradually stir in milk. Bring to a boil, stirring constantly, then lower heat until thickened. Stir a little of hot mixture into beaten egg; return to hot mixture. Bring just to the point of boiling. Cool, then chill in refrigerator. With spoon, beat chilled mixture, then fold in whipping cream and vanilla. Pour into piecrust. Prepare glaze by combining strawberries and water in saucepan; cook 2 minutes then strain through sieve. In saucepan, mix ¼ cup sugar and 2 teaspoons cornstarch; gradually add berry juice. Cook, stirring constantly, until thick and clear. You may choose to add color with red food coloring. Spread glaze over cream mixture in piecrust. Sliced strawberries may be added for garnish. Chill before serving.

Polly Kuhns, Dunnegan, MO

Strawberry Cream Cake Roll

Cake:

4 eggs	¾ cup sifted cake flour
1 teaspoon vanilla	1 teaspoon baking powder
¾ cup sugar	¼ teaspoon salt

In mixing bowl, beat eggs and vanilla on high speed for 5 minutes or until lemon colored. Gradually add sugar, beating until dissolved. Combine flour, baking powder, and salt; fold gently into egg mixture just until combined. Pour into jelly roll pan lined with wax paper. Spread batter evenly over pan. Bake at 375 degrees for 10 to 12 minutes or until light brown. Turn out onto a cloth that has been sprinkled with powdered sugar. Peel off paper from cake. Roll up cloth and cake. Let cool.

Cream Filling:

1 cup whipping cream	½ teaspoon vanilla
¼ cup sugar	2 cups frozen or fresh strawberries, cut up

Whip cream, sugar, and vanilla. Unroll cake and spread filling over it. Sprinkle with strawberries. Roll up cake again and chill for 2 hours before serving. Sprinkle with powdered sugar. Cut 1-inch slices. Garnish with additional strawberries and whipped cream, if desired.

Lizzie Schrock, Sullivan, OH

Zucchini Brownies

4 eggs
1½ cups oil
2 cups sugar
2 cups flour
2 teaspoons baking soda
2 teaspoons cinnamon

1 teaspoon salt
4 tablespoons cocoa
1 teaspoon vanilla
4 cups shredded zucchini
1 cup chopped nuts

Beat together eggs, oil, and sugar. Sift together flour, baking soda, cinnamon, salt, and cocoa; add to egg mixture and blend well. Add vanilla, zucchini, and nuts. Spread onto greased and floured 10 x 15-inch jelly roll pan. Bake at 350 degrees for 30 minutes. Good served plain or frosted.

Mrs. Andy L. Schlabach, Spencer, OH

Sweet Potato Pie

2 cups cooked mashed sweet
   potatoes
1 (14 ounce) can condensed
   sweetened milk

2 large eggs
1 tablespoon vanilla
¼ teaspoon salt
1 unbaked piecrust

Mix and beat all ingredients except piecrust until smooth. Pour into piecrust. Bake at 350 degrees for 60 minutes.

Sharri Noblett, Memphis, TX

Soft Zucchini Bars

2 cups sugar
1¼ cups oil
4 eggs
2 cups flour

2 teaspoons baking soda
1 teaspoon salt
1½ teaspoons cinnamon
2⅛ cups grated zucchini

Mix sugar, oil, and eggs. Add flour, baking soda, salt, and cinnamon. Fold in zucchini. Spread into greased jelly roll pan. Bake at 350 degrees for 20 minutes.

Frosting:

6 ounces cream cheese
¼ cup butter

2 teaspoons vanilla
1½ cups powdered sugar

Combine ingredients and beat until smooth. Spread over cooled bars.

Judy Wengerd, Monroe, IN

BUNDT ZUCCHINI CAKE

3 eggs
1 cup oil
1½ cups sugar
3 cups flour
1 teaspoon cinnamon
½ teaspoon salt
1 teaspoon baking soda
1 teaspoon baking powder

1 cup shredded coconut
1 cup chopped nuts or
  chocolate chips
1 cup drained crushed
  pineapple
2 cups peeled and grated
  zucchini
Powdered sugar

Blend eggs, oil, and sugar. Combine flour, cinnamon, salt, baking soda, and baking powder; add to egg mixture. Stir in remaining ingredients. Pour into greased and floured Bundt pan. Bake at 325 degrees for 1 hour and 13 minutes. Let cake set 10 minutes before removing from pan with a few shakes. Cool on rack. When cooled, dust with powdered sugar.

Mary H. Miller, Heuvelton, NY

ZUCCHINI PIE

3 cups shredded zucchini
1 cup sugar
3 tablespoons flour
1 teaspoon cinnamon
1 teaspoon butter, melted

1 unbaked piecrust
¾ cup flour
½ cup brown sugar
⅓ cup butter

Combine zucchini, sugar, 3 tablespoons flour, cinnamon, and butter; place in unbaked piecrust. Mix topping of ¾ cup flour, brown sugar, and butter; sprinkle on top of zucchini mixture. Bake at 400 degrees for 10 minutes; reduce to 350 degrees until set and inserted knife comes out clean.

Mary Schwartz, Stanwood, MI

Zucchini Carrot Cake

2 cups flour	¾ cup vegetable oil
2 cups sugar	4 eggs
2 teaspoons cinnamon	1 teaspoon vanilla
½ teaspoon salt	2 cups shredded zucchini
1 teaspoon baking powder	1 cup shredded carrots
2 teaspoons baking soda	

Combine flour, sugar, cinnamon, salt, baking powder, and baking soda. Add oil, eggs, and vanilla; mix well. Fold in zucchini and carrots. Pour into greased 9 x 13-inch pan and bake at 350 degrees for 45 minutes. When cool, frost with cream cheese frosting.

Cream Cheese Frosting:

½ cup butter, softened	1 teaspoon vanilla
1 (8 ounce) package cream cheese, softened	1 cup chopped pecans (optional)
3½ cups powdered sugar	

Cream butter and cream cheese together. Add powdered sugar and vanilla; beat until smooth. Fold in nuts.

Mrs. Levi Miller, Sr., Clark, MO

Zucchini Lemon Drops

½ cup butter, softened
1 cup sugar
1 egg
1 cup finely shredded
  zucchini
2 teaspoons lemon flavoring

2 cups flour
1 teaspoon baking soda
1 teaspoon baking powder
1 teaspoon cinnamon
½ cup raisins
½ cup chopped nuts

In bowl, cream together butter, sugar, and egg. Add zucchini and lemon flavoring. Combine flour, baking soda, baking powder, and cinnamon; gradually add to first mixture. Fold in raisins and nuts. Drop by teaspoonfuls on greased cookie sheets. Bake at 375 degrees for 8 to 10 minutes until lightly browned. Glaze.

Lemon Glaze:

2 cups powdered sugar

2 to 3 tablespoons lemon juice
  (or use half lemon flavoring
  and half water)

Mix sugar and lemon juice well, until spreadable.

Esther Keim, Ashland, OH

Chocolate Bean Cake (Gluten Free)

2 cups cooked beans of choice (black, pinto, navy), rinsed
6 eggs
¾ cup sugar or honey
1 teaspoon vanilla
¼ cup oil
½ cup cocoa powder
2 teaspoons baking powder
½ teaspoon salt
1 teaspoon baking soda

Blend together beans, eggs, sugar, and vanilla until thoroughly incorporated. Add oil, cocoa, baking powder, salt, and baking soda; mix well. Bake in greased pan at 350 degrees for 25 to 30 minutes.

Mrs. Peter Landis, Brodhead, WI

Walnut Coffee Cake

3 cups wheat flour
¾ cup honey
5 teaspoons baking powder
12 tablespoons butter
2 teaspoons cinnamon
1½ cups milk
2 eggs
1½ teaspoons salt
2 teaspoons vanilla

Mix all ingredients together and pour into greased cake pan.

Topping:

½ cup honey
4 tablespoons butter
4 teaspoons cinnamon
1 cup chopped walnuts

Combine ingredients and cover cake batter. Swirl in using a knife. Bake at 375 degrees for 20 minutes.

Fran Nissley, Campbellsville, KY

Recipes for Snacks and Extras

*O taste and see that the L*ORD *is good:*
blessed is the man that trusteth in him.

Psalm 34:8

Berry Parfait

4 cups quick oats
2 cups brown sugar
1 cup butter, melted
Strawberries

Blueberries
1 quart vanilla yogurt
8 ounces whipped topping

Mix together oats, brown sugar, and butter. Spread on cookie sheet. Toast at 300 degrees for 20 to 30 minutes. Cool and break apart. Layer granola, fruit, and yogurt in clear bowl or cups. Top with whipped topping.

Leanna Keim, Sugarcreek, OH

Apple Oatmeal Pancakes

2 cups buttermilk or sour
   milk
2 cups old-fashioned oats
2 eggs, divided
¼ cup oil (I use coconut)
½ cup spelt flour
½ teaspoon salt

1 teaspoon baking soda
1 teaspoon baking powder
½ teaspoon cinnamon
2 tablespoons molasses or
   honey
1 apple, chopped

Start the night before by soaking buttermilk and oats together. The next morning, add egg yolks and oil. In separate bowl, combine flour, salt, baking soda, baking powder, cinnamon, molasses, and apple. Gently combine wet and dry mixtures until just moistened. Beat egg whites until stiff and fold into batter. Fry on hot griddle with oil. If batter is too thick, thin with milk.

Phebe Peight, McVeytown, PA

Candied Apples

5 to 6 cups water
5 ounces cinnamon candies,
   approximately

2 to 3 drops red food coloring
8 apples, pared and halved

Bring water, candies, and food coloring to a boil in large heavy kettle until mixture becomes syrup. Place apples in syrup. Cook, turning only once. Add more candies as apples cook. Judge readiness by color of apples. Cook 1 layer of apples at a time. Boil remaining syrup down to jelly—it is ready when it fills the prongs of a cold fork. Pour some jelly over apples. Store remainder in glass jar for later use on bread and butter. Serves 8 to 16.

Fruit Dip

8 ounces cream cheese
8 ounces sour cream
½ cup strawberry jam
2 tablespoons lemon juice

Blend cream cheese and sour cream together. Add jam and juice, mixing well. Serve with fresh fruit. Apple slices work very well.

Regina Gingerich, Beattie, KS

Caramel Dip for Apples

1 (8 ounce) package cream cheese
½ cup plus 2 tablespoons brown sugar
1 teaspoon vanilla

Beat all ingredients together and refrigerate. Serve with apple slices.

Irene Mast, Kalona, IA

Very Good Fruit Glaze

1 quart water
½ cup Clear Jel
1¼ cups sugar
1 teaspoon vanilla
1 teaspoon butter
Gelatin (your choice of color and flavor)

Bring water to a boil. Mix Clear Jel and sugar; add a little water. Pour into boiling water and bring back to boiling. Add vanilla, butter, and enough gelatin to give glaze color. Let cool. Pour over any mixture of fresh fruit.

Mrs. Freeman Yoder, Millersburg, OH

Cauliflower Bean Dip

1 head cauliflower	1 teaspoon salt
1 can cannellini (white kidney) beans, drained and rinsed	1 teaspoon thyme
	2 teaspoons cumin
	⅓ cup lemon juice
3 cloves garlic	¼ cup olive oil

Roast cauliflower (covered) in oven at 350 degrees for 1 hour. Blend cauliflower with remaining ingredients in blender or food processor. Serve with corn chips or crackers.

Anna M. Byler, Belleville, PA

Refrigerator Pickles

6 cups thinly sliced
   cucumbers
2 cups sugar
1 cup white vinegar
1 tablespoon salt

1 teaspoon celery seed
   (optional)
1 cup sliced green pepper
1 cup sliced onion

Mix all ingredients together, cover, and refrigerate. Ready to eat in 24 hours. These will keep for a long time. Can also be frozen.

Rose Marie Shetler, Berne, IN

Mary Ann Yutzy, Bloomfield, IA

Fermented Dill Pickles

INGREDIENTS FOR ONE QUART:

1 grape leaf
Cucumbers, whole or cut
1 tablespoon chopped fresh
   dill or 1 teaspoon dill seed
½ teaspoon garlic powder

3 to 4 drops stevia liquid
   (optional)
1 tablespoon Celtic sea salt
4 tablespoons whey

Put grape leaf on bottom of jar then fill with cucumbers. Add other ingredients and fill with water. Screw lid on tightly and shake to mix. Note: Grape leaves are said to add crispness, but they are optional. Let stand at room temperature for 3 days then place in cold storage (refrigerator or cellar). Don't use for 10 days. These taste a lot like hamburger dills.

Joni Miller, Brown City, MI

CREAMY CUCUMBER DIP

8 ounces cream cheese
1 cup sour cream
2 tablespoons salad dressing (or mayonnaise)
½ teaspoon Worcestershire sauce
1 medium cucumber, chopped
¼ cup green pepper, chopped
1 rounded tablespoon onion, chopped

Mix together first 4 ingredients, then add chopped veggies. Refrigerate 2 hours. Serve with crackers.

Vonda Yoder, Middlebury, IN

Cucumber Spread

1 cucumber, chopped
1 small onion, chopped

1 (8 ounce) package cream
cheese, softened

Place cucumber and onion in blender or food processor; puree. Drain most of the juice from vegetables through strainer, then blend vegetables into cream cheese. Refrigerate for at least 12 hours before serving on crackers or party rye bread.

Salad Dressing

1 cup ketchup
1 cup salad oil
1 cup sugar

½ cup vinegar
½ teaspoon powdered
mustard

Blend all ingredients together; put into bottle and shake to incorporate. Optional: Add onion, green pepper, etc. Best served over fresh tomatoes, but also good on other raw vegetables.

Alma Gingerich, Irvona, PA

Fresh Salsa

1 cup chopped onion
2 jalapeño peppers
6 cups chopped tomatoes
1 tablespoon oil

1 tablespoon vinegar
1 tablespoon salt
½ tablespoon cumin
½ teaspoon minced garlic

Put onion and peppers through food processor to mince. Combine with remaining ingredients. Serve fresh with chips.

Mary Ann Yutzy, Bloomfield, IA

FRIED BLOSSOMS

Flowers from squash,
    pumpkin, lilies, dandelion
Egg, beaten

Flour
Oil

Take flowers, unwashed, and dip into egg; roll in flour. Fry in oil; turning to brown both sides. They will puff up and taste a bit like mushrooms.

Alma Gingerich, Irvona, PA

RAW TOMATO RELISH

8 pounds ripe tomatoes,
    peeled and chopped
6 medium bell peppers, finely
    chopped
6 medium onions, finely
    chopped

1 cup salt
1 quart white vinegar
3½ cups sugar
1 teaspoon celery seed
1 teaspoon mustard seed

Mix together tomatoes, peppers, onions, and salt. Let stand for 1 hour; drain well. Combine vinegar, sugar, celery seed, and mustard seed, stirring until sugar dissolves. Add to tomato mixture. Store in glass jars in refrigerator. Keeps several months. Good with potato haystacks, meats, rice dishes, and more.

Mrs. Paul Schrock, Salem, MO

Stuffed Jalapeño Peppers

18 jalapeño peppers
1 clove garlic, pressed
1 (8 ounce) package cream
   cheese, softened
1 cup shredded cheddar
   cheese

¼ cup mayonnaise
½ teaspoon oregano
2 egg whites
1 tablespoon milk
2 cups crushed cornflakes

Cut each pepper in half lengthwise and remove seeds and membranes.
Mix garlic, cream cheese, shredded cheese, mayonnaise, and oregano.
Whisk egg whites and milk together. Stuff peppers and dip in egg-milk
mixture. Roll in cornflakes. Place on cookie sheet and bake at 375 degrees
for 30 minutes or until peppers are tender.

Lorene Lehman, Middlebury, IN

Pepper Poppers

1 pound bacon	1 (8 ounce) package cream
Sweet banana or hot peppers	cheese
	½ cup shredded cheddar cheese

Fry bacon; cut in small pieces. Halve peppers; remove all seeds and wash thoroughly. Mix bacon, cream cheese, and cheddar cheese together. Fill pepper halves with mixture. Set peppers in 9 x 13-inch pan and cover with foil. Bake at 400 degrees for 30 minutes.

Mrs. Mahlon (Nancy) Miller, Middlefield, OH

Hot Pepper Wraps

Hot peppers
¼ cup chopped onion
Oil

¼ pound hamburger
1 pint pizza sauce
Bread dough

Remove all seeds from inside of hot peppers. Fry onion in a little oil; add hamburger. Fry a little then add pizza sauce. Fill hot peppers with hamburger mixture. Wrap with your favorite kind of bread dough and put in cake pan. Bake at 350 degrees until done.

Wollie Schlabach, Smicksburg, PA

Onion Rings

1 large sweet onion
Oil
⅔ cup milk

⅔ cup flour
1 teaspoon baking powder
½ teaspoon salt

Cut onion into ½-inch rings. Heat oil deep enough for frying to 350 degrees. Beat together milk, flour, baking powder, and salt. Dip rings into batter. Deep fry until golden brown. Serve with ketchup.

Mrs. Samuel Gingerich, Danville, OH

CUCUMBER PUNCH

3 quarts water
3 quarts ice cubes
1 (14 ounce) package sugar-free instant lemonade powder
1 (12 ounce) can white grape juice concentrate
1 lemon, sliced
½ medium cucumber, thinly sliced

In punch bowl, stir together water, ice, lemonade powder, and grape juice concentrate. Float slices of lemon and cucumber on top.

GINGER ALE

¾ cup ginger, peeled and finely grated or chopped
½ cup lime juice
¼ to ½ cup maple syrup or other sweetener
2 teaspoons salt
¼ cup whey
2 quarts water

Place all ingredients in 2-quart jug. Stir well and cover tightly. Leave at room temperature for 2 to 3 days. Strain and refrigerate. Put about ⅓ to ½ cup ale in a glass and fill with water. Serve.

Anna Zook, Dalton, OH

MAMA'S RED RASPBERRY BREW

½ gallon raspberry leaves
3 cups alfalfa herb
3 cups peppermint leaves
2 cups nettle leaves

Blend ingredients. To make tea, add 2 to 3 teaspoons of mixed herbs to 1 cup boiling water. Steep 2 to 3 minutes. Strain and add honey to taste.

Anna Zook, Dalton, OH

HAY-TIME SWITCHEL

Thought to originate in the West Indies during the 1600s, switchel made its way to the American colonies and became a popular drink to revive thirsty farmers.

2 cups sugar
1 cup molasses
¼ cup apple cider vinegar

1 teaspoon ground ginger
1 gallon water, divided

Heat sugar, molasses, vinegar, and ginger in 1 quart water until dissolved. Add remaining water; chill and serve. Yields 1 gallon.

Mollie Stolzfus, Charlotte Hall, MD

Recipes for Preserving the Harvest

*Blessed shall be the fruit of thy body, and the fruit
of thy ground, and the fruit of thy cattle, the
increase of thy kine, and the flocks of thy sheep.
Blessed shall be thy basket and thy store.*

Deuteronomy 28:4–5

A WORD of CAUTION about CANNING

These recipes are contributed by home cooks and may not necessarily follow professional guidelines for the canning process and time. The editors have attempted to make correct recommendations and caution in choice of recipes.

Know your equipment. If you are unfamiliar with the canning process, consider taking a class from a local group. The Ball Canning site often lists links to classes at www.freshpreserving.com/community/classes.

For further education, go to The National Center for Home Food Preservation website at http://nchfp.uga.edu/. The US Department of Agriculture's *Complete Guide to Home Canning* is the ultimate resource for home canning. It is available to download for free, chapter by chapter, at the USDA's website.

The canning process can fail, and the food can spoil and sicken those who consume it. So learn how to troubleshoot. If you question your ability to master canning, skip it and choose to consume your produce quickly or freeze it. And when you're in any doubt of the age or quality of your canned goods, throw them out.

General Canning Steps

1. Prepare jars, using only approved canning jars. Clean in hot water. Examine jars for any cracks or chips. Discard those.
2. To sterilize canning jars without having to dip them into boiling water—which can be dangerous—wash the jars and place upside down in the oven. Heat oven to 250 degrees and "bake" for 20 minutes.
3. Prepare your product (vegetable, fruit, soup, etc.) according to the recipe.
4. Fill jars to the neck (or shoulder), leaving space so the product does not touch the lid.
5. Wipe jar rims clean.
6. Heat brand-new lids according to manufacturer's instructions. Never reuse jar lids for canning.
7. Set lids on rims and screw down with ring bands. Bands can be reused, but not the flat lids.
8. Process in either a pressure canner or a water bath, according to recipe directions and manufacturer's instructions. Generally, a water bath (also called cold packing when the contents are cold or uncooked) is used for high-acid foods like pickles, tomatoes, fruits, jellies, sauerkraut, etc. Pressure canning is recommended for low-acid foods and most vegetables, soups, meats, dairy products, etc.
9. Remove jars to cool on a rack for 12 or more hours.
10. Check lid seal while removing bands. Flat lids should make a popping sound in the process of sealing and concave down. They should not move in the center when touched, and finger pressure should not pop the lid off.
11. Label with the contents and date of processing. Store in a cool, dark place like a basement and use within one year.
12. Before use, check that the seal is still holding firm. Look for mold or strange bubbles. Check for any bad smell. If in doubt, throw it out. Never taste the canned food cold (unless pickled). Always boil low-acid foods for 10 to 20 minutes before tasting.

Fruit Canning Tips:

- ◆ Syrup for Canning Fruit
- ◆ Heavy syrup: 1 cup sugar to 1 cup water
- ◆ Medium syrup: 1 cup sugar to 2 cups water
- ◆ Light syrup: 1 cup sugar to 3 to 4 cups water

When canning sweet cherries, use light syrup. Too much sugar makes them wrinkle.

A light syrup of 1 cup sugar and 4 cups water is plenty sweet for peaches.

Add vitamin C powder to applesauce when canning to retain its yellow color. We add no sugar.

Elizabeth Shetler, Brinkhaven, OH

CANNED APPLES

4 quarts shredded or sliced   1 cup sugar
   apples

Layer apples and sugar in bowl and let sit overnight. Next morning, stir well and put into jars. Cold pack 10 minutes; let sit in water another 10 minutes before removing to cooling rack. Use as you would fresh apples in your favorite recipes, but reduce sugar as apples are already sweetened.

Edith Mast, Bertha, MN

APPLE PIE FILLING

12 quarts peeled and chopped apples	2 cups honey
¾ cup flour	1 tablespoon cinnamon
	1 tablespoon nutmeg

Mix all ingredients together and pack into quart jars. Fill jars with water to replace air spaces. Process in water bath for 30 minutes.

Fran Nissley, Campbellsville, KY

APPLE PIE FILLING #2

10 cups water	½ cup butter
2 cups brown sugar	2¼ cups Perma-flo, mixed into a paste with a little water
4 cups sugar	
2 teaspoons cinnamon	
3 tablespoons lemon juice	3½ quarts chopped or sliced apples
1 tablespoon salt	

In pot, bring water, sugars, cinnamon, lemon juice, and salt to a boil; add butter. Stir in Perma-flo paste and return to boiling. Remove from heat and add apples. You can run apples through food mill. Pour into jars; set lids. Cold pack 10 minutes in hot water bath. Yield: 6 quarts.

Susie Miller, Patriot, OH

FRUIT PIE FILLING

8 cups water
4 cups sugar
2 teaspoons salt
½ cup lemon juice
1 cup Clear Jel
9 cups fruit

Bring water, sugar, salt, and lemon juice to a boil; add Clear Jel. Fold in fruit. Pour into jars and process in hot water bath for 10 minutes.

Anna Yoder, Laurenceberg, IN

PIE FILLING

1½ cups water
¾ cup sugar
2 heaping tablespoons Perma-flo
⅓ cup gelatin (flavor of your choice)
Dash salt
1 tablespoon lemon juice
1½ to 2 cups fruit of your choice

Boil water and sugar. Thicken with Perma-flo. Add gelatin. Remove from heat and add salt, lemon juice, and fruit. Pour into jars, set lids, and seal in hot water bath for 30 minutes. It can also be frozen.

Joanna Williams, Guthrie, KY

MIXED FRUIT

Fill 8-quart bowl with mixture of chunked watermelon, muskmelon (cantaloupe), and pineapple. Coat with 1 cup of sugar. Pack into jars, set lids, and cold pack for 15 minutes.

Mrs. Abe Miller, Patriot, OH

Black Raspberry Pie Filling

12 pints raspberries
30 cups water
9 cups sugar
5 cups Perma-flo

4 cups water
9 tablespoons lemon juice
4½ teaspoons salt

In pot, bring berries, water, and sugar to a boil. Add remaining ingredients. Cold pack in jars for 5 minutes. Yield: 14 quarts. Use to fill pies and pastries.

Sharon Mishler, Lagrange, IN

CANTALOUPE

Cantaloupe
2½ cups sugar
4 cups hot water
¾ cup vinegar

½ teaspoon stevia powder (or double the sugar)
½ teaspoon salt
4½ cups pineapple juice
1½ cups lemon juice

Pack melon pieces into jars. Dissolve sugar in water. Add remaining ingredients. Pour over melon to fill jars. Process in hot water bath for 15 minutes. Note: Use only good, firm melons. Soft fruit will turn to mush when canned.

Mrs. Joseph (Martha) Miller, Gallipolis, OH

Cantaloupe #2

12 quarts cantaloupe, cut in
  chunks
1 quart pineapple juice
2 cups sugar

¾ cup lemon juice
1 tablespoon salt
2 (20 ounce) cans chunked
  pineapple

Mix all ingredients together and pack into jars. Set lids and seal in hot water bath for 30 minutes.

Thelma Zook, Oakland, MD

Peaches

2 (46 ounce) cans pineapple
  juice
2 cans frozen orange juice
  concentrate

2 gallons water
Peaches, peeled and sliced
Stevia powder

Mix juices with water. Fill quart jars with peaches. Add ¼ teaspoon stevia powder to each jar. Fill jars with juice. Set lids and pressure can for 8 minutes.

Regina Gingerich, Beattie, KS

Peach Marmalade

5 cups mashed peaches
7 cups sugar
2 cups crushed pineapple

1 (6 ounce) package gelatin
(peach, apricot, orange, or
raspberry)

Combine peaches, sugar, and pineapple in saucepan. Boil for 15 minutes. Add gelatin and stir until dissolved. Pour into jars and seal.

Linda Fisher, Leola, PA

Grape Juice and Grape Filling

Concord grapes, fresh and ripe

Pick grapes off stems and wash grapes. Put grapes in juicer/steamer. Steam grapes, stirring once, until no more juice comes out–about 45 to 50 minutes. Put pulp through food strainer, using the grape auger. Results will be separated into mush and juice.

Juice:

Fill jars with juice. Process quarts in boiling water for 10 minutes. To fix juice to drink, mix 1 quart grape juice, 2 quarts water, 1 teaspoon pure white stevia powder (or sugar to taste), and ice to make 1 gallon.

Filling:

1 quart water
1¾ cups sugar
⅔ cup Perma-flo
1½ tablespoons black raspberry gelatin
1 quart grape mush

Bring water to a boil. Remove from heat. Mix together sugar, Perma-flo, and gelatin; stir into hot water. This will not get lumpy if sugar and Perma-flo are properly mixed. Stir in grape mush. Mix well. Fill jars. Process quarts in boiling water for 20 minutes. Delicious served on top of cereal.

Mrs. Thomas Beachy, Liberty, KY

Grape Juice

Bring 6 cups water and 4 cups grapes to a boil; drain juice. Add sugar to taste. To seal in quart jars, process in water bath for 15 minutes.

Cevilla Swartzentruber, Navarre, OH

Grape Butter

4 cups grapes, crushed   4 cups sugar

Combine grapes and sugar and let set overnight. Place in saucepan and cook for 20 minutes; put through sieve. Bring mixture back to a boil. Pour into jars and seal.

Mrs. Levi Gingerich, Dalton, OH

Ukrainian Grape Juice

For extra delicious grape juice, place 3 to 4 slices of apple in bottom of each jar. Add grapes until ⅓ full; fill with water. Process in water bath to seal. There is no need for sugar, and it is deliciously different. We learned this is how they do it in Ukraine.

Phebe Peight, McVeytown, PA

Apple Butter

24 cups applesauce
8 cups sugar
1 cup vinegar
1 tablespoon cinnamon

¼ teaspoon allspice
¼ teaspoon cloves
¼ teaspoon salt

Mix all ingredients together and put in oven at 250 degrees until brown and thick. Makes 9 pints to process and seal.

Mary Alice Yoder, Topeka, IN

Old-Fashioned Apple Butter

Pour 6 gallons sweet apple cider in outdoor kettle. Make a mark on a clean stick to show how deep the cider is in the kettle. Add 4 gallons more cider. When cider has boiled down to 6-gallon mark, add 8 gallons apple snitz (peeled slices). Do it slowly so cider doesn't stop boiling. Cook until snitz are pudding-like in consistency. Keep stirring well, especially after snitz are added. Blend 2 quarts sugar (more or less depending on sweetness of apples), 6 teaspoons cinnamon, and ¾ teaspoon salt; add to apple butter. Pour into jars; seal in water bath 5 to 10 minutes.

Alvin and Katie Hertzler, Salisbury, PA

Apple Peel Jelly

Apple peels
5 cups water
Cinnamon stick (optional)

1 (1.75 ounce) box pectin
7 cups sugar

Lightly pack apple peels into 4- or 5-quart pot with 5 cups water. Bring to a boil for 15 minutes, stirring as little as possible. Remove from heat; add cinnamon stick. Put lid on pot and let stand overnight. Strain apple liquid into measuring cup; make sure you have 5 cups. Place liquid in separate pot and heat. Gradually add pectin, stirring until dissolved; bring to a full rolling boil over high heat. Add sugar, stirring to dissolve. Return to boiling for 1 minute. Remove from heat and skim foam if necessary. Pour into jars and seal in hot water bath.

Anna Yoder, Fairchild, WI

MOCK PINEAPPLE

1 gallon peeled, seeded, and diced zucchini	1 (48 ounce) can pineapple juice
1½ cups lemon juice	3 cups sugar

Bring all ingredients to a boil and simmer 20 minutes. Pour into jars and process in hot water bath for 30 minutes.

Anna Yoder, Fairchild, WI

RED BEET JELLY

12 large beets, approximately	½ cup lemon juice
7 cups water	8 cups sugar
2 (1.75 ounce) packages Sure-Jell	1 (6 ounce) package raspberry gelatin

Peel beets and simmer in water for 30 minutes. When beets are tender, strain off liquid; it should yield 6 cups of beet juice. Save beets for another recipe. Combine juice, Sure-Jell, and lemon juice in saucepan and bring to a boil. Add sugar all at once and heat to boiling. Boil for 5 minutes. Remove from heat. Add gelatin and stir until dissolved. Pour into sterile jars and seal in water bath for 5 to 10 minutes after water comes to a boil.

Clara Miller, Fredericktown, OH

DANDELION BLOSSOM JELLY

1 quart dandelion blossoms
5 cups water

1 (1.75 ounce) package Sure-Jell
4 cups sugar

Wash and remove all green from blossoms. In large saucepan, place water and blossoms; boil for 5 minutes then drain, retaining liquid. To liquid, add Sure-Jell and sugar. Cook until thickened and coats a spoon.

Yellow Pear Tomato Preserves

5 cups yellow pear tomatoes

6 cups sugar

1 (3 ounce) package lemon gelatin

1 (3 ounce) package apricot gelatin

Wash tomatoes and cut into halves; place in saucepan. Add sugar and bring to a hard boil for 15 minutes. Add gelatin and stir until dissolved. Pour into sterile jars and seal in water bath for 5 to 10 minutes after water comes to a boil.

Sharri Noblett, Port Arthur, TX

Rhubarb Juice

18 pounds rhubarb stalks, coarsely cut
4 cans frozen orange juice concentrate
2 quarts pineapple juice
1 cup maple syrup
2 teaspoons stevia powder (or to taste)

Steam rhubarb for 2 hours or until colorless and dry. (I use a Nutri Steamer.) Put rhubarb juice in stockpot or large bowl and add remaining ingredients. Pour into jars, set lids, and cold pack in hot water for 10 minutes. Serve over ice cubes or add to cold water for a refreshing drink.

Mrs. Andy Hershberger, Navarre, OH

Green Tomato Jam

2 cups grated green tomatoes
2 cups sugar
1 (3 ounce) package gelatin, any flavor (I like raspberry)

Bring tomatoes and sugar to a rolling boil for 20 minutes. Add gelatin. Refrigerate or can into jars.

Elizabeth Miller, Brown City, MI

GREEN BEANS

Fill quart jars with snapped and washed green beans. To each jar add: 2 tablespoons vinegar, 1 tablespoon sugar, and 1 teaspoon salt. Fill jars with water; set lids. Process in hot water bath for 30 to 60 minutes. Adding vinegar and sugar keeps the beans from spoiling when using the hot water bath method, and they are still nice and firm. I find that the beans are still a bit too crunchy for our preference when they are processed for only 30 minutes, so I do mine for 60 minutes.

Rachel Troyer, Millersburg, OH

GREAT NORTHERN OR PINTO BEANS

Put 1¼ cups dry beans in quart jars. Fill with water and let stand for 12 hours or more. Add 1 teaspoon salt to each jar. Pressure can for 25 minutes at 10 pounds pressure.

Shirley Schlabach, Crofton, KY

DILLY BEANS

2 cups vinegar
2 cups water
3 tablespoons canning salt

2 pounds green beans, approximately
Garlic
Dill seed
Red pepper flakes (optional)

Prepare syrup of vinegar, water, and salt in pot, bringing it to a boil. Clean green beans and pack raw whole beans into pint jars so beans are standing up. To each jar add 1 clove garlic, ½ teaspoon dill seed, and ½ teaspoon red pepper flakes. Pour syrup over beans to fill jars almost to the top. Set lids and process in hot water bath for 10 minutes. Ready to use in 2 to 3 weeks.

PICKLED RED BEETS

Beets
7 cups water
7 cups sugar
2½ cups vinegar

½ teaspoon ground cloves
2 teaspoons cinnamon
½ teaspoon pepper
2 tablespoons salt

Cook beets in water; remove and reserve water. Peel and cut beets. Pack into jars. Dissolve sugar in water and add vinegar and seasonings. Pour into jars to fill. Cold pack for 30 minutes to seal.

Mrs. Joseph (Martha) Miller, Gallipolis, OH

Red Beets

4 quarts beets	2 teaspoons whole allspice
3 cups vinegar	2 to 3 sticks cinnamon
2 cups water	½ teaspoon whole cloves
2½ cups sugar	1 teaspoon salt

Cook beets until just tender and skins slip off. Discard skins. Combine vinegar, water, sugar, spices, and salt. Bring to a boil and simmer 15 minutes. Add beets to syrup and simmer 5 minutes. Pack beets into jars. Return syrup to a boil and pour over beets. Set lids and seal in hot water bath.

Joanna Williams, Guthrie, KY

Pickled Corn

4 cups vinegar	½ head cabbage, finely chopped
1 cup sugar	2 ripe bell peppers, finely chopped
1 tablespoon salt	
8 cups fresh corn (about 12 ears), cut from cob	1 tablespoon celery seed
	1 tablespoon mustard seed

In large kettle, combine vinegar, sugar, salt, and corn; bring to a boil. Add cabbage, peppers, celery seed, and mustard seed; return to a boil and cook for a few minutes. Pour into jars, set lids, and process in hot water bath for 15 minutes.

Lydia Schwartz, New Auburn, WI

Cinnamon Cucumber Pickles

2 gallons (approximately
   7 pounds) extra large
   cucumbers, peeled, cored,
   and sliced ½-inch thick
2 cups lime
7 cups vinegar, divided

1 tablespoon alum
1 bottle red or green food
   coloring
10 cups sugar
8 sticks cinnamon

In large bowl or crock, soak cucumbers in 2 gallons water with lime for 24 hours. Drain and rinse well; place in large saucepan. Combine 1 cup vinegar, alum, and food coloring. Pour over cucumbers and add water to cover cucumbers. Heat and simmer for 2 hours. Drain and place in bowl. Make syrup with 6 cups vinegar, 2 cups water, sugar, and cinnamon; bring to a boil. Pour syrup over cucumbers and let stand overnight. Drain and reheat syrup; pour back over cucumbers and let stand overnight. Do this for 3 days. On third day, pack cucumbers with syrup in pint jars and seal.

Hot Garlic Dill Pickles

Cucumbers
Fresh dill
Garlic cloves
Hot peppers

3 quarts water
1 quart vinegar
1 cup salt

Slice cucumbers or use small whole ones. Pack into quart jars. To each jar, add 1 head fresh dill, 1 clove garlic, and 1 hot pepper. You can adjust the heat by cutting peppers and using only one half per jar. Bring water, vinegar, and salt to a boil. Pour into jars. Process in hot water bath to seal jars.

Phebe Peight, McVeytown, PA

GARLIC DILL PICKLES

Small cucumbers
2 cloves garlic or 1 teaspoon
   garlic powder per quart
1 head dill or 2 tablespoons
   dill seed per quart

2 cups water
2 cups vinegar
3 cups sugar
2 tablespoons salt

Slice cucumbers and fill quart jars to the neck. Add garlic and dill to each
jar. Heat water, vinegar, sugar, and salt. Fill jars with liquid. Set lids and
process in hot water bath to the boiling point. Turn off heat and let set 5 to
10 minutes, then remove jars from water. Ready to eat in 2 weeks.

Levi and Clara Troyer, Loganville, WI

Kosher Dill Pickles

Cucumbers
¼ teaspoon powdered alum
   per jar
1 clove garlic per jar
1 grape leaf per jar
1 or 2 heads dill per jar

⅛ teaspoon cayenne pepper
   or 1 hot pepper per jar
3 quarts water
1 quart vinegar
Scant ¾ cup salt

Use whole little cucumbers or slice and cut larger cucumbers to your preferred size. Pack into 7 or 8 quart jars. Into each jar, add alum, garlic, grape leaf, dill, and cayenne pepper. In pot, bring water, vinegar, and salt just to the boiling point. Prepare your canner with hot water that will be ready at the same time as the syrup. Pour syrup over cucumbers to fill jars. Seal in hot water bath for 10 minutes. I turn my jars upside down on the counter to cool so they will seal better.

Mrs. Joseph (Martha) Miller, Gallipolis, OH

Million-Dollar Pickles

6 quarts small cucumbers	2 cups water
6 medium onions, sliced	2 tablespoons mustard seed
½ cup salt	1 tablespoon celery seed
3 cups vinegar	6 cups sugar

Combine cucumbers, onions, and salt; let stand overnight with enough water to cover. Drain. In saucepan, mix vinegar, water, mustard seed, celery seed, and sugar. Bring to a boil. Pack pickles in jars; pour syrup over top. Set lids and seal.

Mattie Yoder, Fairchild, WI

Our Favorite Pickles

Cucumbers, sliced	4 cups sugar
1 cup pickling lime	3 tablespoons salt
1 gallon water	3 cups water
4 cups apple cider vinegar	1 tablespoon Kosher Dill Mix

For crisp pickles, soak cucumber in lime and water for 1 to 2 hours. Rinse well. Pack cucumbers into jars. Combine vinegar, sugar, and salt with 3 cups water. Pour into jars. Process in water bath for 10 minutes.

Rebecca T. Christner, Bryant, IN

SWEET DILL PICKLES

Cucumbers, sliced
Garlic
Dill
2 cups vinegar

2 cups water
3 cups sugar
2 tablespoons salt

Pack sliced cucumbers into 6 pint jars. Add 1 clove or ¼ teaspoon minced garlic and 1 head of fresh dill to each jar. Bring vinegar, water, sugar, and salt to a boil. Pour over cucumbers to nearly fill jars. Seal with lids and place jars in hot water bath. Bring water to a boil, then turn off heat. Remove canner lid. Let stand to cool before removing jars. Ready to eat in about 2 weeks.

Mrs. Allen (Miriam) Keim, Patriot, OH

Iva Troyer, Apple Creek, OH

Mary Ann Yutzy, Bloomfield, IA

SWEET PICKLE STICKS

Cucumbers
3¾ cups vinegar
6 cups sugar
3 tablespoons canning salt

4½ teaspoons celery salt
4½ teaspoons turmeric
¾ teaspoon mustard seed

Clean cucumbers and remove any noticeable seeds. Cut into sticks. Place in pan and cover with boiling water. Let stand 12 hours. Drain cucumbers and pack into jars. Combine remaining ingredients for syrup. Bring to a boil for 5 minutes. Pour into jars over cucumbers. Makes enough syrup for 10 pints. Process to seal in water bath for 5 to 6 minutes. Wait 2 weeks before consuming.

Mrs. Freeman Yoder, Millersburg, OH

Sweet Mustard Pickles

Cucumbers, sliced or chunked
Celery seed
Salt
Mustard seed
Onion, sliced

Prepared mustard (optional)
6 cups sugar
3 cups water
3 cups vinegar
1 teaspoon turmeric

Prepare 5 to 6 quart jars. Fill each with cucumbers; add 1 teaspoon celery seed, 1 teaspoon salt, 1 teaspoon mustard seed, 1 sliced onion, and ¼ teaspoon prepared mustard to each jar. Cook sugar, water, vinegar, and turmeric into a syrup; pour over cucumbers. Seal and cold pack jars in water to the boiling point. Remove canner from heat and let stand 15 minutes before removing jars from water.

Miriam Hershberger, Apple Creek, OH

Hot Pepper Butter

40 jalapeño peppers, diced	1 tablespoon salt
2 cups mustard	1 cup flour
1 quart vinegar	½ cup water
6 cups sugar	

Mix jalapeños, mustard, vinegar, sugar, and salt and bring to a boil. Add flour mixed with water to mixture. Boil for 5 minutes. Pour into jars and seal. Use as dip for chips and on sandwiches.

Katie W. Yoder, Goshen, IN

CANNED PEPPERS

Clean peppers, cut into strips or squares as desired, and pack in jars. Add 1 teaspoon vegetable oil and 1 teaspoon salt to each quart jar. Syrup: 1 pint vinegar; 3 cups water; 3 cups sugar. Mix and pour over peppers while boiling hot. Seal. Cold pack to the boiling point.

Mrs. Gideon M. Miller, Norwalk, WI

CANNING HOT PEPPERS

Hot peppers	4 teaspoons salt
3 quarts water	1½ cups sugar
1 quart vinegar	1 teaspoon turmeric

Pack peppers into sterile jars. Bring remaining ingredients to a boil. Pour over peppers. Seal with lids. Turn jars upside down several hours until sealed, or cold pack in hot water for 5 to 10 minutes.

Mrs. Joseph Schwartz, Salem, IN

Pickled Zucchini

Zucchini
Salt
7 cups sugar
2½ cups water

5 cups vinegar
Turmeric
Pickling spice

Cut zucchini into sticks; soak overnight in salt water. Fill jars with zucchini sticks. Mix sugar, water, vinegar, turmeric, and pickling spice in pot; bring to a boil until sugar dissolves. Fill jars with liquid to 1 inch from top. Cold pack in hot water for 5 to 7 minutes.

Joe and Tina Eicher, Hudson, KY

Chow Chow

1 large head cauliflower, chopped
1 quart chopped cucumbers
1 quart chopped carrots
1 quart cut green beans
1 quart lima beans
1 quart corn

1 pint chopped green pepper
1 pint chopped red pepper
1 pint tiny onions
3 cups sugar
1½ tablespoons dry mustard
1 quart vinegar
1 pint water

Cook each vegetable separately in salted water to desired tenderness, but not too soft. Drain veggies and mix them together. In large pot, combine sugar, dry mustard, vinegar, and water; bring to a boil. Add veggies and return to boiling point. Pack into jars and process in hot water bath to seal.

Amanda M. Miller, Apple Creek, OH

Chow Chow #2

1 medium head cabbage
6 medium onions
6 green peppers
6 sweet red peppers
4 cups green tomatoes
¼ cup salt
2 tablespoons prepared
mustard

6 cups cider vinegar
2½ cups sugar
1½ teaspoons ground
turmeric
1 teaspoon ginger
2 tablespoons mustard seed
1 tablespoon mixed pickling
spices

Clean and chop all vegetables. Place in 1-gallon crock. Add salt and mix well. Cover; let stand 12 to 18 hours at room temperature. Drain. In 6-quart kettle, blend prepared mustard and vinegar with wire whisk. Add sugar, turmeric, ginger, and mustard seed. Tie pickling spices in cheesecloth bag and add to kettle. Bring to a boil. Simmer uncovered for 20 minutes. Add vegetables. Simmer uncovered for 10 minutes. Remove spice bag. Ladle into 8 hot pint jars.

Anna Yoder, Laurenceberg, TN

Harvesttime Mixed Pickles

2 quarts lima beans
2 quarts green beans, cut
1 quart kidney beans
1 quart chopped celery
1½ quarts chopped carrots
6 red peppers, chopped
6 green peppers, chopped
2 large heads cauliflower, remove florets and cut into bite-size pieces
Salt

2 quarts chopped cucumbers
1 quart chopped onion
1 quart cooked small shell macaroni
10 cups sugar
4 cups vinegar
8 cups water
1 teaspoon cinnamon
4 teaspoons celery seed
2 tablespoons turmeric
2 tablespoons Clear Jel

In separate pots, cook beans, celery, carrots, peppers, and cauliflower in a little salted water until just tender. Drain. Combine cooked vegetables, cucumbers, onion, and macaroni. Mix brine of sugar, vinegar, water, cinnamon, celery seed, turmeric, and Clear Jel. Pour over vegetables. Pack into jars with lids. Cold pack for 30 minutes.

Esther Keim, Ashland, OH

MIXED PICKLE RELISH

1 gallon chopped cucumbers
1 gallon chopped carrots
1 gallon chopped peppers
  (sweet green, red, yellow)
1 gallon chopped cabbage
2 quarts green beans
1 quart kidney beans
1 quart navy beans
1 quart chopped onion
2 quarts whole kernel corn

2 bunches celery, finely
  chopped
1 pint water
2 pints apple cider vinegar
10 cups sugar
2 tablespoons turmeric
3 tablespoons dry mustard
4 teaspoons salt
1 cup flour

Cook all vegetables separately until tender, then combine in large container and mix well. In 6-quart kettle, mix water, vinegar, sugar, turmeric, mustard, and salt. Bring to a boil. Mix flour with enough water until it is thin enough to pour into boiling mixture; stir well and return to boiling. Pour over vegetables. Mix well. Put into quart jars with lids and cold pack for 45 minutes to seal.

Lydia C. Yoder, Chetopa, KS

ZUCCHINI VEGETABLE MIX

4 quarts unpeeled zucchini, cubed
6 medium onions, chopped
2 cups diced carrots, cooked
2 cups diced celery, cooked
2 heads cauliflower pieces, cooked
4 red peppers, chopped

½ cup salt
5 cups sugar
1½ teaspoons turmeric
1½ teaspoons celery seed
1 teaspoon garlic salt
2 cups vinegar
1 cup water

Mix all vegetables together with salt and cover; let stand for 3 hours at room temperature; drain. Mix sugar, turmeric, celery seed, garlic salt, vinegar, and water together and pour over vegetables and boil for 5 minutes. Seal in jars.

Joni Miller, Brown City, MI

SANDWICH SPREAD

20 medium carrots
10 red peppers
10 green peppers
2 onions
12 green tomatoes

1 cup prepared mustard
1½ cups sugar
1 tablespoon celery seed
3 quarts salad dressing

Grind all vegetables together. Put into cloth bag and drain for 1 hour. Place drained vegetables in large saucepan and add mustard, sugar, and celery seed; bring to a boil for 10 minutes. Remove from heat; add salad dressing (best if at room temperature). Seal into jars.

Petie and Katie Schwartz, Galesburg, KS

Winter Slaw

2 cups shredded cabbage
2 green peppers, chopped
1 red pepper, chopped
1 large carrot, sliced

1 pint vinegar
2½ cups sugar
¼ teaspoon turmeric
½ teaspoon salt

Prepare vegetables in large bowl. Combine vinegar, sugar, turmeric, and salt; pour over vegetables. Pack into jars. Process in water bath for 20 minutes.

Laura Brenneman, Stanwood, MI

Apple Relish

16 cups cored and ground apples	2 cups ground hot red peppers (jalapeño or other)
8 cups ground onion	8 cups vinegar
	12 cups sugar

Grind apples, onion, and peppers. Combine all ingredients and cook in large kettle until thickened. Simmer for 45 minutes to 1 hour, stirring constantly. If mixture becomes dry, add a little more vinegar. Skim off foam. Pour into sterilized jars and seal in hot water bath for 10 minutes.

Sharri Noblett, Port Arthur, TX

Sweet Cucumber Relish

4 quarts ground cucumbers	Crushed ice
6 onions, ground	3 cups vinegar
1 green pepper, ground	4 cups sugar
1 red pepper, ground	1½ teaspoons turmeric
⅓ cup salt	1½ teaspoons celery seed
1 teaspoon alum	2 tablespoons mustard seed

Put ground vegetables in large crock, sprinkle with salt and alum, and top with crushed ice. Set for 3 hours; drain. Combine vinegar, sugar, turmeric, and seeds. Bring to a boil. Pour into jars with lids. Seal in hot water bath for 10 minutes.

Levi and Clara Troyer, Loganville, WI

Green Tomato Relish

4 cups chopped onion	6 cups sugar
12 green peppers	1½ teaspoons turmeric
4 cups chopped green tomatoes	2 cups water
4 cups ground cabbage	1 tablespoon celery seed
6 red peppers	2 tablespoons mustard seed
Salt	4 cups vinegar

Grind all vegetables with coarse blade. Sprinkle with salt and let set overnight. The next day, rinse and drain. Combine with other ingredients and heat to simmer for 3 minutes. Put into jars and seal.

Katie Bontrager, Middlebury, IN

Onion Relish

1½ gallons ground onion
½ cup salt
1 quart cider vinegar

4½ cups sugar
1 teaspoon turmeric
1 teaspoon pickling spice

Mix onion and salt; let stand 30 minutes. Squeeze juice from mixture and discard juice. To onion, add vinegar, sugar, turmeric, and pickling spice. Bring to a boil and cook 30 minutes, stirring often. Pour into jars, set lids, and process in hot water for 10 minutes.

Levi and Clara Troyer, Loganville, WI

Sweet Pepper Relish

12 medium red or yellow
   peppers
3 medium onions
1½ cups cider vinegar
1½ cups sugar

1 tablespoon pickling salt
1 tablespoon mustard seed
2 tablespoons celery seed
2 tablespoons minced garlic

Clean and chop peppers and onions. Mix vinegar, sugar, salt, and spices. Add to vegetables; mix well. Bring to a boil over medium heat. Boil for 25 to 30 minutes or until thickened. Stir to prevent sticking. Fill jars, set lids, and process in hot water bath for 15 minutes.

Thelma Zook, Oakland, MD

PICKLE RELISH

18 small cucumbers, coarsely
  ground
1 quart ground onion
12 bell peppers, coarsely
  ground
1 cup salt

3 cups sugar
3 cups vinegar
1 teaspoon turmeric
1 teaspoon celery seed
1 teaspoon mustard seed

Bring cucumbers, onion, peppers, and salt to a boil for 15 minutes; drain well. Add remaining ingredients. Bring to a full boil. Pack into jars with lids. Seal in hot water bath for 10 minutes.

Fannie Miller, Lakeview, MI

Salsa

14 cups chopped tomatoes
3 cups chopped onion
2 cups chopped green pepper
½ cup chopped hot peppers
8 ounces tomato paste
½ cup sugar

½ cup vinegar
3 tablespoons salt
1 tablespoon garlic powder
1½ teaspoons cumin
1 tablespoon cilantro
5 tablespoons instant Clear
Jel or arrowroot

Mix all ingredients and pack into jars without cooking. Process in hot water bath for 20 minutes. Yields 9 to 10 pints.

Phebe Peight, McVeytown, PA

THICK AND CHUNKY SALSA

14 pounds tomatoes (scalded, peeled, chopped)
5 cups chopped onion
6 green peppers, chopped
¾ cup vinegar
1½ cups brown sugar
¼ scant cup salt
1 teaspoon garlic powder
2 teaspoons oregano
3 teaspoons cumin
3 teaspoons chili powder
1 (4 ounce) package Mrs. Wages Mild Salsa Mix
10 tablespoons Clear Jel

Combine all ingredients except Clear Jel. Boil for 45 minutes. Stir Clear Jel into a little water to make a paste before adding it to salsa to thicken. Cold pack in jars for 20 minutes. Yields 16 pints.

Luella Miller, Shreve, OH

ZUCCHINI RELISH

10 cups shredded zucchini
4 cups chopped onion
2 cups shredded carrots
5 tablespoons salt
1 red pepper, chopped
1 green pepper, chopped
2½ cups vinegar
3 cups sugar
2 tablespoons cornstarch
1 teaspoon turmeric
2 teaspoons dry mustard
2 teaspoons celery seed
½ teaspoon pepper

Mix zucchini, onion, carrots, and salt; refrigerate overnight. Rinse and drain vegetables, then put into kettle. Mix remaining ingredients and add to zucchini mixture. Boil until thickened; stirring frequently. Ladle into jars. Process in hot water bath for 10 minutes. Makes 7 to 8 pints.

Doretta Yoder, Topeka, IN

Salsa Spicy

10 cups tomato juice
4 cups chopped onion
3 cups chopped sweet
  peppers
1½ cups diced hot peppers
4 tablespoons chopped garlic
5 tablespoons vinegar
5 tablespoons sugar

3 tablespoons oregano
3 tablespoons salt
3 tablespoons pepper
2 tablespoons olive oil
2 tablespoons Worcestershire
  sauce
1 tablespoon dill weed
5 tablespoons Perma-flo

Heat tomato juice to the boiling point; add all remaining ingredients except Perma-flo. Add Perma-flo and cook until slightly thickened. Yields 1 gallon. Pack in jars; seal in water bath for 15 minutes.

Fannie Stutzman, Dalton, OH

Barbecue Sauce

4 quarts tomato juice
¾ cup ReaLemon juice
2¾ cups Worcestershire sauce
½ cup salt
3½ cups vinegar
10 cups brown sugar
¾ cup mustard

⅓ cup paprika
⅔ cup liquid smoke
½ tablespoon garlic powder
½ tablespoon black pepper
½ tablespoon red pepper
4 onions, chopped
3 cups Perma-flo

Mix everything but Perma-flo, and cook for 20 minutes. Thicken with Perma-flo. Put in jars and cold pack for 10 minutes.

Katie Bontrager, Middlebury, IN

Six-Day Ketchup

½ bushel ripe tomatoes
¼ cup salt
1 cup vinegar
4 to 5 cups sugar
¼ cup mixed pickle spice

3 medium onions, chopped
½ large green pepper, chopped
¼ cup cornstarch or Perma-flo
½ cup water

Slice unpeeled tomatoes and layer into large crock with salt between layers. Place a light weight (like a dinner plate) on top of tomatoes. Let stand 5 days in cool place like cellar. On sixth day, drain liquid off thoroughly. Run tomatoes through sieve. Put tomatoes, vinegar, and sugar in pot. In a cloth bag, put spice, onions, and green pepper and tie shut. Place bag in tomato mixture and cook for 45 minutes. Remove bag and squeeze liquid into mixture. Make a smooth paste of cornstarch and water. Add to tomatoes and cook for 10 minutes. Pack into jars with lids. Seal in hot water bath for 10 minutes.

Fannie Mast, Gamlier, OH

Levi and Clara Troyer, Loganville, WI

MANDY'S SPAGHETTI SAUCE

1 bunch celery
3 large onions
4 bell peppers
4 hot peppers
½ bushel tomatoes, after
   going through a sieve, or 10
   quarts tomato juice
⅔ cup salt

2 teaspoons pepper
3 teaspoons garlic salt
1 cup vegetable oil
2 cups sugar
2 teaspoons Worcestershire
   sauce
1 quart tomato paste

Chop vegetables into stockpot filled with tomato juice. Add salt, pepper, garlic salt, oil, sugar, and Worcestershire sauce. Cook until thickened–about 3 hours. Thin tomato paste with some of hot tomato juice; add to pot during last 30 minutes of cooking. Pour into jars; seal. Process in hot water bath for 10 minutes.

Mrs. Eli (Amanda) Hershberger, Navarre, OH

APPLE KETCHUP

6 apples	½ teaspoon mustard
8 quarts tomatoes	½ teaspoon ground cloves
3 large onions	½ teaspoon cinnamon
4 cups sugar	1½ cups vinegar
3 tablespoons salt	½ cup water

Cook apples, tomatoes, and onions until soft. Drain extra juice. Put through food mill. Combine with remaining ingredients; boil for 10 minutes. Pour into jars and cold pack for 10 minutes.

Amanda Schwartz, South Whitley, IN

KETCHUP

2 gallons tomato juice	½ tablespoon ground cloves
2 cups vinegar	7 tablespoons salt
2 onions, minced	8 cups sugar
1 tablespoon cinnamon	9 tablespoons Clear Jel
½ tablespoon allspice	

Boil tomato juice, vinegar, onions, cinnamon, allspice, cloves, and salt for 30 minutes to 1 hour to reduce, then add sugar. Combine Clear Jel with a little water to make a paste and add. Pour into pint jars and process in hot water bath for 10 minutes.

Brenda Yoder, Topeka, IN

Marinara Pizza Sauce

9 quarts tomato juice
4 bell peppers, chopped
9 onions, chopped
8 celery stalks, chopped
1 gallon tomato paste
1 quart ketchup
3 tablespoons chili powder
9 tablespoons paprika

3 tablespoons garlic powder
6 tablespoons salt
3 tablespoons oregano
3 tablespoons dry mustard
2 tablespoons pepper
2½ cups Parmesan cheese
3 cups sugar

Cook tomato juice, peppers, onion, and celery until vegetables are tender. Put through food mill. Add remaining ingredients and bring to a boil. Pour into jars and cold pack for 30 minutes.

Becky Hershberger, Apple Creek, OH

Tomatoes

Blanch and skin tomatoes. Remove core and any hard spots. Cut into pieces. Stuff into jars up to jars' shoulder. Use butter knife to remove any air pockets. Add 1 teaspoon canning salt to each quart jar. Set lids and process in hot water bath for 30 minutes.

Tomato Juice

7 quarts tomato juice	2 teaspoons onion salt
1 cup sugar	1 teaspoon garlic salt
3 tablespoons salt	¼ teaspoon red pepper
3 teaspoons celery salt	3 teaspoons paprika

Combine all ingredients. Pour into jars and seal in hot water for 20 minutes. Makes a tasty drink or base for chili.

Wilma Yoder, Pulaski, IA

Vegetable Juice

1 peck of tomatoes	1¼ cups salt
4 large onions	1 tablespoon sugar
1 bunch celery, chopped	1 teaspoon pepper
12 sprigs parsley	1 teaspoon basil
2 green peppers, chopped	2 bay leaves
8 carrots, chopped	1 teaspoon whole cloves

Wash tomatoes and do not peel. Cut into pieces. Add remaining ingredients and simmer for 30 minutes. Pour mixture through food mill, then return to pot. Bring to a boil. Pour in hot glass jars and seal.

Rachel Yoder, Burton, OH

Hot Tomato Juice

22 quarts chopped tomatoes
3 to 4 large onions, chopped
2 to 4 bell peppers, chopped
4 jalapeño peppers, chopped

Salt
Garlic Salt
Celery Salt

Cook vegetables until soft. Run through food processor or juicer. To every gallon of juice add 1 heaping tablespoon salt, 1 tablespoon garlic salt, and 1 tablespoon celery salt. Can in water bath for 10 minutes. Tip: Several cloves can be cooked with the vegetables, but if used, omit garlic salt.

Mrs. Raymond Kauffman, Laplata, MO

Tomato Soup

½ bushel tomatoes
4 stalks celery
3 large onions
3 green and/or red peppers

2 carrots
Parsley
Salt, to taste

Chop and cook vegetables in their own juices until very soft. Put everything through blender. (Tomato skins will get pureed.) To seal in jars, process in water bath for 30 minutes. This soup is a good base for other soups and casseroles.

Laura Schwartz, Bryant, IN

Tomato Soup #2

½ bushel tomatoes, chopped
1 large bunch celery, chopped
4 large onions, chopped
1 cup sugar

1 cup butter, melted
1 cup flour
1 tablespoon pepper
Salt, to taste

Cook tomatoes, celery, and onion in large pot for about 1 hour. Run through sieve to separate juice from the solids. Return juice to pot and bring to a boil. Combine sugar, butter, flour, pepper, and salt; add to juice. At this point it may be served, or can jars in water bath for 20 minutes.

Laura Brenneman, Stanwood, MI

Ham, Bean, and Bacon Soup

15 pounds navy beans
7 stalks celery, chopped
4 cups chopped onion
Large bunch parsley, chopped
15 bay leaves
5 teaspoons thyme

6 tablespoons salt
1½ teaspoons pepper
7½ pounds ham, diced
⅛ cup beef base
5½ quarts tomato juice
4½ pounds bacon

Soak beans overnight in water; drain; cover with water and boil. Cook until almost done. In large pot of water, cook celery, onion, parsley, bay leaves, thyme, salt, and pepper for 40 minutes. Add ham during last 10 minutes. Remove bay leaves. Thin beef base with some tomato juice; add to soup along with remaining tomato juice. Fry bacon until crisp. Crumble into soup. Pour into quart jars and set lids. Pressure can at 10 pounds for 30 minutes.

Levi and Clara Troyer, Loganville, WI

Chunky Beef Soup

8 pounds hamburger	4 quarts tomato juice
2 large onions, chopped	½ cup butter
4 quarts sliced carrots	2 quarts beef broth
3 quarts peas	¾ cup beef base
4 quarts chopped potatoes	1¾ cups sugar
2 quarts cut green beans	Salt and pepper
¼ cup salt or less, divided	8 cups flour (or perhaps less)
2½ gallons water	

Brown hamburger with onion. Cook vegetables individually in salted water until just tender; drain. In large pot, heat water, tomato juice, butter, beef broth, beef base, and sugar. Add vegetables to soup. Add hamburger along with pan drippings. Season with salt and pepper to taste. To flour, add enough water to make a smooth paste. Add to boiling soup and stir until thickened. Pour into quart jars and set lids. Cold pack for 2 hours or pressure can at 10 pounds for 40 minutes.

Levi and Clara Troyer, Loganville, WI

Vegetable Soup

1 quart sweet corn
1 quart peas
1 quart chopped carrots
1 quart chopped celery
1 quart chopped onion
2 quarts chopped potatoes
2 bell peppers, chopped
2½ gallons tomato juice
2 tablespoons parsley flakes
Salt, to taste
1 (12 ounce) box alphabet
    pasta

¾ cup brown sugar
1 can pork and beans
1 (1.5 ounce) package
    meatloaf seasoning
1 (1.5 ounce) package beef
    stew seasoning
1 (1.5 ounce) package sloppy
    joe seasoning
1 (1.5 ounce) package chili
    seasoning
1 tablespoon taco seasoning

Cook vegetables in juice until soft. Add parsley and salt to taste. Cook pasta until just softened; strain. Combine all remaining ingredients and add to soup. The seasoning packets are a must as they are what give the soup such good flavor. Makes 20 quarts. Cold pack in jars for 2 hours.

Elizabeth Miller, Brown City, MI

CREAM OF MUSHROOM SOUP

2 (8 ounce) boxes fresh
  mushrooms, chopped
2 pounds butter, melted,
  divided
3¾ cups flour

10 cups water
10 cups whole milk
5 teaspoons salt
5 tablespoons beef soup base

In skillet, sauté mushrooms in some of the butter until tender. In large stockpot, combine remaining butter and flour; add water, milk, salt, and soup base. Boil until thickened; add mushrooms. Pour into ½ pint or pint jars. Pressure can at 10 pounds for 20 minutes. Yields 15 pints. Very handy to have in stock and better than store-bought.

Jolene Bontrager, Topeka, IN

CANNING NUTS

Pecans and other nuts can be canned if you have a lot on hand. Put in dry jars with new lids that seal. Heat oven to 175 to 200 degrees. Lay jars on rack with pecans or other nuts inside with lids on. Add no liquid. Bake for 45 minutes to 1 hour, or when pecans are heated through. Turn oven off and let jars cool on racks. If the temperature is too hot, it will make the nuts brown and taste scorched. If sealed properly, they will taste fresh for up to 1 year.

Lydia Miller, Goshen, IN

Canning Popcorn

You can grow your own popcorn in the garden. In the fall, when stalks are dry and brown, pull off and husk the ears. Break off any tops of the ears that are bad or wormy.

Spread out the ears to finish drying for several weeks. This can be done on a sheet in an upstairs room or attic. To check if the corn is dry enough, shell and pop several ears. If it pops nicely, it is dry and ready to shell. If many of the kernels only pop about halfway and are crunchy instead of fluffy, it needs to dry longer.

Shell the popcorn. Pour shelled popcorn from one bucket to another in front of a fan to blow out all the fuzzy chaff. Repeat several times until popcorn is clean. (Be sure to do this outside!)

Fill jars with popcorn. Put on lids and put jars in the oven. Heat quarts at 225 degrees for 45 minutes. Turn off oven and allow to cool before removing jars from oven.

The popcorn must be heated to keep it from becoming buggy, and then it can be stored for a long time. Even if the lids don't seal, as long as the rings are tight, you will have no problem with bugs.

Another method is to pressure can quarts at 5 pounds for 5 minutes. Do not use a higher temperature, or it will damage your popcorn and it won't pop. Both methods work equally well.

We have been growing our own popcorn for years, and every Sunday evening we enjoy our home-grown, home-canned, freshly popped popcorn.

Mrs. Thomas Beachy, Liberty, KY

PEACHES

1 (16 ounce) can frozen orange
  juice concentrate
2 juice cans full of water

1½ to 2 cups sugar
Peaches

In bowl, mix together juice, water, and sugar. Peel and slice peaches into juice. Freeze with as much syrup to peaches ratio as you like. Syrup keeps peaches from browning.

Susan Byler, Crab Orchard, KY

Regina Gingerich, Beattie, KS

PEARS

4 cups water   Pears
3 cups sugar

Cook water and sugar until sugar is dissolved. Fill freezer jar with diced or sliced pears and cover with syrup so they don't turn brown. You can do peaches the same way.

Using frozen fruit: Dump a jar of frozen strawberries, peaches, and pears into bowl and add can of Sprite and eat while slushy and partly frozen. Very refreshing dessert on a warm summer day.

Betty Miller, Goshen, IN

SLUSH

6 cups sugar   8 bananas, mashed or
6 cups water   chopped
5 (20 ounce) cans crushed   3 cans frozen orange juice
   pineapple   concentrate
4 (15 ounce) cans mandarin   9 quarts chopped fresh
   oranges   peaches

Dissolve sugar in water. Mix everything together and put in freezer containers and freeze. Makes 16 quarts. To serve, allow to thaw slightly before spooning out servings.

Jolene Bontrager, Topeka, IN

Strawberry-Rhubarb Jam

3 cups strawberries, chopped
and drained
4 heaping cups diced rhubarb

4 cups sugar
1 scant cup strawberry
gelatin

Combine strawberries, rhubarb, and sugar; cook 15 minutes. Add gelatin. Freeze or pour into hot jars and seal.

Jolene Bontrager, Topeka, IN

Honey

Put honey in small freezer containers and freeze to prevent sugaring. It thaws fast.

Betty Miller, Goshen, IN

Green Veggies

Add a pinch of baking soda to your water when blanching green vegetables like peas and green beans. They will keep a fresh vibrant green through freezing and cooking.

Christina Peight, Belleville, PA

Beans and Peas

When freezing fresh green beans, peas, or butter beans, first boil them in water for 5 minutes. Cool. Pour vegetables AND water into freezer bag, seal, and freeze. The vegetables will taste much better later and you won't have poured off any of the vitamins.

Anna Byler, Minerva, OH

Popcorn

If kept in freezer, popcorn will have fewer "old maids," or unpopped kernels.

Betty Miller, Goshen, IN

Corn

Clean fresh corn on the cob. Drop into boiling water and cover with lid. Cook for 5 to 7 minutes until kernels have a glassy sheen. Remove from boiling water into pan of cold water. Let cool several minutes. Set corn up to drain in dish drainer. When cool enough to handle, cut off kernels. Don't cut into the cob. Use the edge of the knife to scrape the milk out of the cob. Scoop 2 to 3 cups into freezer bag. Label and freeze flat.

To use as a side dish, thaw corn. Place corn in saucepan with just a little water–perhaps ¼ cup water per 2 cups corn. Add 2 tablespoons butter, ½ teaspoon salt, and if desired, 1 tablespoon sugar. Cook until warmed through; don't allow it to come to a rolling boil.

Index of Contributors

INDEX OF RECIPES BY SECTION

Recipes for Salads

Recipes for Soups

Recipes for Main Dishes

Recipes for Sides

Recipes for Desserts

Recipes for Snacks and Extras

Recipes for Preserving the Harvest

Index by Key Ingredients